DESERT OF DEATH

Leo Docherty was born in Scotland and grew up in Gloucestershire. After studying Swahili and Hindi at university he attended the Royal Military Academy Sandhurst and was commissioned into the Scots Guards in 2001. First posted to London, he performed ceremonial duties and trained as a paratrooper. After a short spell in Germany he completed an Arabic course and served operationally in Iraq.

Having passed a further language course in Pashtu, he deployed to southern Afghanistan as the aide-de-camp to the commander of the first British forces to enter the volatile Helmand Province in April 2006. His language skills quickly led him to move from the British Headquarters to serve alongside the Afghan National Army.

A passionate traveller and linguist, he used his leave periods while serving in the Army to travel extensively in Asia and the Middle East on horseback, bicycle and by public transport. He left the army in December 2006.

LEO DOCHERTY

Desert of Death

A Soldier's Journey from Iraq to Afghanistan

faber and faber

First published in 2007
by Faber and Faber Limited
3 Queen Square London WC1N 3AU

Typeset by Faber and Faber Ltd
Printed in England by Mackays of Chatham plc,
Chatham, Kent

A CIP record for this book
is available from the British Library

978-0571-23837-8

10 9 8 7 6 5 4 3 2 1

This book is dedicated
to the soldiers still serving in Iraq and Afghanistan

My sincere thanks to Bob and Margaret Docherty, Abi Docherty, Paddy Docherty, Susie Hyde-Smith, Bessie Kelaart, Hannah and Billy Woollen, Thierry Kelaart, Henry Volans and Neil Belton. – L.D.

Contents

Afghanistan and Helmand Province

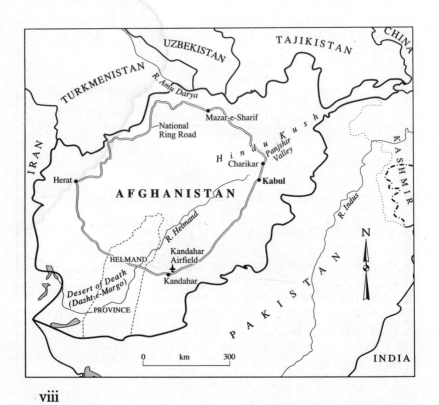

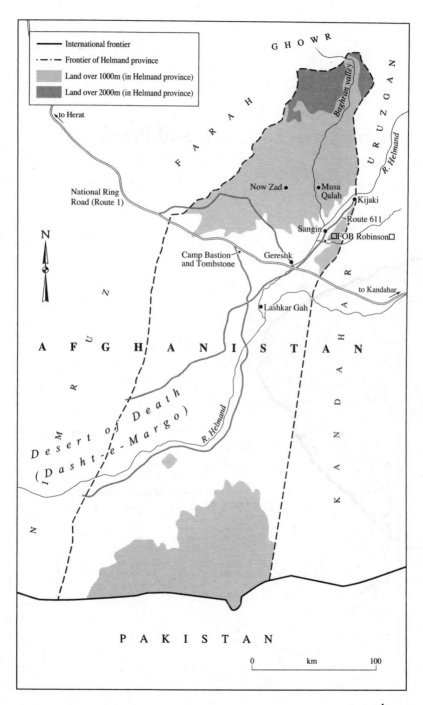

Illustrations

All photographs courtesy of the author.

Preface

Hurriedly striding out of Wellington Barracks, I check my watch again.

'Fuck!' I exclaim in a whisper. I'd better get a move on; I'm due to the see the Major General in ten minutes, and must be there at least five minutes beforehand.

Cutting a diagonal through the gaudy flower beds of St James's Park, I reset my tie knot, button my suit jacket and draw my shirt cuffs over my wrists. Despite my haste I'm feeling pretty smart in my favourite grey suit, cut like an hourglass, with ultra-sharp trouser creases, and – thanks to my old orderly, Guardsman Lambe – my shoes are like black glass. The finishing touch is a couple of inches of pink silk handkerchief floating out of my breast pocket; a bit of dash will go down well with the Major General.

Darting out of the path of a black cab, I cross the road, onto the gravel of Horse Guards Parade, heading towards the main building: a great white stone edifice, ancient and solid. This is the headquarters of the Major General, commander of all the troops in London. Crunching across the vast parade ground I survey its fringes: the nondescript rear of

Downing Street, Mountbatten's bronze effigy clutching binoculars, and a pair of mounted stone generals, rigidly upright on each flank of the empty square.

As I walk under the archway in the centre of the vast building, I pause beside a cavalry trooper, ceremoniously guarding the entrance in a blue cape and white-plumed metal helmet, and press the door buzzer. The trooper looks a bit peeved to be dismounted, unlike his mate on the White-hall side of the archway who's getting all the attention on his colossal 'cavalry black' war horse.

In the Aide-de-Camp's cramped office I'm ushered to a sofa, to wait for the call to see the Major General in the adjoining room, behind a tall oak door. I struggle to dry my sweat-sodden palms on the sofa cushion, not that I'm expecting to be shaking hands. Having already been formal-ly charged with misconduct I'm about to find out what my punishment will be; the best-case scenario is that I get a ver-bal reprimand, the worst case that I'm court-martialled, fined and dishonourably discharged without pension. How-ever, as I'm leaving the Army anyway, if the Major General kicks me out I wouldn't much care. My greatest worry is that he'll deprive me of my leave by ordering me to do duties in London for the next couple of months.

The ADC, an earnest Irish Guards officer, answers inces-sant phone calls at a desk littered with paper. He's basically a diary assistant to the Major General. It's his first day in the job and he's flustered but resolutely good humoured. The atmosphere is a little awkward; he's junior to me but I'm here for a bollocking, which seems unnatural for us both.

'Could you get Captain Docherty a cup of tea please?' he

asks the secretary in between phone calls. She agrees cheer-fully, perhaps glad for the chance of a fag break.

Drinking my tea and sweating into the sofa, I wait to see the General.

I used to be a soldier: a Captain in the Scots Guards, a tradi-tional, blue-blooded Foot Guards regiment. Late last year, having served in Afghanistan, I publicly expressed my opin-ion of the campaign and caused an almighty furore in the media. As a serving officer, I was punished by the Army for breaking the rules. But now I'm out; I'm a civilian, at liberty to speak, to look back on the journey that's led me via Iraq, London and Afghanistan to the Major General's door.

I'm not a journalist or a writer. Unlike TV news and print media this is a *soldier*'s true account of being on the ground at the very centre of the British campaign in Helmand at its inception. This is a version of events that hasn't yet been told. It does not seek praise; better stories will come of heroic brav-ery and courageous endurance, and also greater understand-ing. This, the first word, will surely be followed by a deluge.

I never imagined that I'd speak publicly or write about my time in the Army. The military culture of reticence and obe-dience stifles honest, reflective expression. Leaving the Army doesn't make it any more natural, because in a way, you *never* leave; military culture doesn't get removed with the uniform. I would therefore deny any charge of disloyalty. It would be disloyal to those still serving in Iraq and Afghanistan *not* to speak. Only silence would be contemptible.

I was in Afghanistan at the beginning of the new war. This is my story.

CHAPTER 1

In the Desert

Fumbling, I unclip the torch from my webbing vest and wave the little red light frantically towards the Chinook beating down onto the helicopter landing site before me. Ideally I'd have it on a bit of string and whirl it around my head, spinning a red 'O' for the pilot to see, but I've been crashed out for this operation, without time to prepare properly, so I just wave it optimistically back and forth.

The Chinook looms down, huge and black. Grains of sand deflect off the tips of the giant twin rotors and burst into green sparks, generating a pair of vast fiery halos, bristling in the darkness.

The loadmaster replies to my light with his own red torch, waving me onboard. I run through the deafening storm of the downdraught, up the tailgate and into the helicopter. I flop down on the canvas seats and buckle in as we pull up hard, my chin forced into my chest. Craning my head, I can see the lights of Sha'iba Logistics Base fading as we make a rapid ascent.

I'm chuffed to bits to be getting out of camp. All I know is that I'm needed as an interpreter for an operation being carried out by 45 Commando Royal Marines. The normal interpreter is on leave, so I've been offered up as a stand-in.

Within a few minutes we descend into the Az Zubayr Port complex, a few kilometres south-east of Sha'iba, on the Shatt Al Arab waterway, where the Marines are based. I'm picked up on the landing site and taken straight into the Orders Group – a meeting in which a commander gives his men their orders for an operation and on a map or model explains how the plan will work.

The company commander, a Major in his late thirties, has the officers and senior non-commissioned officers gathered around him. They've already done rehearsals so these orders are for just for confirmation. The Major has a tough, angular face, deep brown, and dark thinning hair. He runs through the plan in a conversational manner: 'As you already know we're out early doors tomorrow to arrest some people connected with the transit of suicide bombers into Iraq from Saudi . . . They have a Thuraya satellite phone . . . Intelligence has picked up the signal, so this is the key to locating them . . . It's also what we need to find on the objective, which will probably be a Bedouin tent . . .'

The company will be in three main groups: a break-in group, an inner cordon and an outer cordon. The break-in group will go directly to the tent and arrest and search its occupants, while the cordon groups will prevent anyone escaping. I'm to go with the Major in his little command group and be ready to move to the break-in group when called forward.

'This is Captain Docherty. He's the 'terp,' the Major says, nodding in my direction.

I blurt a greeting and add, 'I've done a *short* course,' trying to indicate that I'm not exactly qualified for this, but no one really seems bothered. This op sounds like more of a linguistic challenge than I had anticipated. It is a potential interrogation, not a 'meet and greet'. I now realise why it's too sensitive a mission to use a local interpreter.

After the Major has finished and answered a couple of questions, the wiry Company Sergeant-Major (CSM) gives a few admin details. We're to carry our morphine in the left-hand trouser pocket, so that everyone knows where it is if we take casualties; Zap numbers (the first two characters of your last name and the last four digits of your Army number) are to be marked on the front of body armour, and we're to carry a twenty-four-hour ration pack and as much water as possible.

The men assembled around the map-covered table, with well-worn notebooks, bronzed faces and battered combats, exude the sanguine confidence of those constantly on operations. This is the most exciting thing that I've done so far in Iraq but they're all very used to it; some of the 'bootnecks' – the Marine private soldiers – have done three or four operational tours already in as many years of service. This is my first tour, and I'm delighted to be on operations at last. When I left Sandhurst almost three years ago my regiment, the Scots Guards, had just returned to London from Northern Ireland. Bursting with physical fitness and enthusiasm, I was gutted to find myself marching around in a bearskin and tunic outside Buckingham Palace while my contemporaries in other regiments were in the Balkans, Afghanistan and Sierra Leone. After more than a year inside the M25 the low point came with missing out on Operation Telic 1: the invasion of Iraq in March 2003. With disgusted envy I watched events unfold on the Officers' Mess television.

Now on Operation Telic 5 I've finally got my chance to do something interesting. I did a ten-week basic Arabic course in the spring and I'm pleased this seems to be opening doors. I'm really hoping to get out and about and see some action. I especially like the idea of working closely with the Iraqis, and secretly want to become fluent in their language. I know it makes me unusual as a soldier but I'm passionate about Arabic. During the course I ventured into a Lebanese music shop in London's Edgware Road and bought a cassette of narrated Holy Qur'anic verses. Though ignorant of their meaning, I found the words beguiling and wanted to know more.

Onboard a pair of Chinooks we depart just after dawn the following morning. We make a brief touchdown at the main British headquarters in Basra to collect a couple of Americans – a short pale Sergeant, wearing gloves and wraparound sunglasses, runs up the tailgate, followed by a tall black Major. They're jammed in among the Marines opposite me. The Sergeant's got proper ear-defenders while the Major, like me, has spongy little yellow earplugs which must be compressed and jammed into the ear canal. The visceral turbo-whining and shaking of the engines numb us. The Marines are well used to it, most sleeping over their weapons, rested barrel-down onto the floor. Corporal Fox next to me dozes open-mouthed.

After two hours we make a smooth descent onto the tarmac of an Italian-run Forward Air Refuelling Point (FARP).

Because of the fuel hazard, we have to disembark on the hot gravel next to the runway. The Marines sit listlessly on their patrol packs. The sky is a cloudless pale blue and the sun is ferocious; we're truly in the middle of the desert now.

The American Sergeant is the arresting officer; this operation must have been of US origin in Baghdad. He's come personally for the sake of sound evidence: the same arresting officer must be present with any arrestee from the point of arrest to the courtroom. He gives me the official line that I must tell anyone being arrested the legal jargon about 'being detained for questioning . . . you're not a prisoner'. I reckon I can probably get the gist across, and the Sergeant doesn't seem fussy anyway.

The Major is an artilleryman currently working in the US intelligence department. As a bureaucratic staff officer he rarely gets out of camp: 'I can't believe I'm doin' this shit . . . I'm from an Air Defence unit, they won't believe it when I tell them.'

He makes notes in tiny writing on a square pad; he needs to recall everything in chronological order in case it's required as evidence. I ask him when the Falluja offensive is going to start; I've heard rumours of a massive US operation to rid the northern town of its Sunni insurgents, who've held sway there and across the 'Sunni Triangle' since the spring.

'Today, man. That place gonna be levelled.'

Back on board I look up a couple of words from the official statement in my mini Arabic dictionary. It fits neatly into one of the smaller pouches on my webbing vest – a waistcoat of small pouches. My mind wanders to the memory of purchasing it in Damascus during my recent summer leave: three weeks spent practising my newly learnt Arabic, drinking tea amid a cacophony of backgammon dice, and exploring the bazaars around the Umayyad Mosque.

I'm shaken from my daydreaming as the 'five minutes to go' signal – an open raised palm with fingers splayed – is passed down our seated line. Helmets are replaced and weapons cradled more firmly. I loop my rifle sling over my head and draw a gulp of water from my water satchel, trapping the mini-tap carefully in a zip-up pocket. The 'one minute to go' signal comes. Out of the porthole I can see the desert floor race past, a flat beige blur no more than twenty metres below.

A bump rocks us in unison towards the pilot: we're on the ground, trundling forward, the tailgate lowering into a swirl of dust. Belts are flung off as the helicopter shudders to a halt. Springing to life, we haul ourselves upright and run towards the light and dust at the tailgate. The sand whips my face as I follow the lumbering figure in front of me. The Chinook rotors fade. I can hear my own panting breath, amplified until I extract my yellow ear plugs.

Coming to a halt, we go down on one knee. We're surrounded by hard, flat desert, featureless except for a low black tent about a hundred metres away towards which the break-in group are now sprinting. In front of me is the company commander and Corporal Fox, his signaller. He swings his backpack off his shoulder and extracts an antenna. As he folds out its spiky arms it takes form like a short black metallic Christmas tree. It's the secure VHF radio link back to headquarters in Basra. He's got another radio with a short fat antenna, like a truncheon; this is the UHF set which he uses to speak to the helicopter.

Over the Personal Role Radio (PRR) jammed to my left ear, the break-in group asks for me. I run forward towards the tent.

Outside, a few metres apart from one another, two small men in long white shirts sit cross-legged with their hands on their heads. Wispy black beards and tousled hair poke out from under broad blindfolds. Their small dark bodies and thin limbs look almost fragile. Their tent is a long, low construction of scruffy black cloth, open along one side. Inside, two women huddle with a pair of young children and a baby among a ramshackle collection of cooking implements, grimy bundles of cloth, sacks of flour and a couple of dusty carpets. The Marine searchers are steadily working through it, wearing plastic gloves as a forensic precaution.

'Ask them if they've any weapons, would you, boss,' says the Sergeant in charge of the searching team.

Kneeling down, I ask one of the men, speaking close to his ear.

'Yes,' he replies, shaking with fright. 'We have guns in the tent, for protection.'

At the same moment one of the Marines finds a weapon under one of the carpets. The bundles of cloth and the possessions around them are quickly scattered. The stash of weapons consists of a new but slightly rusty Kalashnikov, a replica of a German G3 rifle, a rusted old Lee Enfield of Second World War vintage and a little pistol. There's also a plastic bag of mixed ammunition: it's clearly just for their personal protection.

'Ask if they have a Thuraya phone,' says the American Major, pausing from his furious note-taking. Unsurprisingly, they say they don't.

While the searchers get really busy dismembering the tent's contents I continue the interrogation, relaying questions from the American Major. Agitated with fear, they garble their replies: they're brothers, their father's dead, their mother and a wife are in the tent, they don't know of any satellite phone . . .

The American Sergeant grows impatient: 'Ask him if he knows about Abu Ghrayb prison,' he says, keen to shock out something incriminating.

I relay the question but it falls flat. It holds no meaning. A silence follows, and the steam has gone out of the interrogation. It seems our detainees are a poor Bedouin family unrelated to the trafficking of suicide bombers. It's baffling because we've been specifically targeted onto this location by the intelligence people in headquarters. Perhaps whoever it was using the Thuraya has already packed up and left.

Sensing that we're onto the wrong people, the American Major has the two detainees moved into a slim band of shade skirting the tent. The Marines half-heartedly start re-constituting its contents, silently watched by the two women. The wife, wearing a tatty party dress, jogs the baby on her arm, her face partly hidden under a head scarf. The old woman, her mother-in-law, is swaddled in a large black gown, tight about her head, that leaves her face exposed. Tiny tattoo dots are just visible amongst the deep lines of her face. Like faded blue tear drops they dot her chin, forehead, cheeks and nose in rough symmetry. The other children burrow silently into her side. On their little shirts, rows of sequins and embroidery glint out from under a layer of grime.

We've now been here for a good hour. Some of the Marines get a photo with the weapons. The American Sergeant joins them. 'This is nothing,' he says, now resigned to not making an arrest. 'I got more weapons 'n that in my house anyway.'

The Chinook beats across the sky and comes down nearby. The two men are helped to stand and have their blindfolds removed. Blinking, they smile fearfully, still uncertain if the ordeal is over.

'We're very sorry to have troubled you,' I shout over the helicopter's roar, feeling a complete shit.

'Thank you, thank you,' they stammer, shaking my hand repeatedly.

As we retreat towards the helicopter, the old woman gains confidence and berates me. I can't understand her words. The men try to calm her.

'I'm sorry,' I shout, turning away and running for the Chinook. I plunge again through a wall of face-stinging dust, heat and noise, and sprawl onto the metal floor as we power upwards.

I'm dehydrated and nauseated by the helicopter's turbo engine whining. I've already drained my water satchel and have lost my yellow earplugs. The heli is packed with blokes now. I'm in a tangled mass of sweating Marines on the floor. Exhausted, we're quietly tolerant of one another.

I'm feeling a bit guilty about the last hour or so, especially as the unfortunate Bedouin were so magnanimous. It was clearly an intelligence cock-up. In a way, though, I'm relieved that it was the wrong target, as a deeper interrogation would have been beyond my linguistic means. Using my fingers I struggle to keep the noise out, shut my eyes and submit to a piercing headache.

Landing again at the Italian base, we're disgorged onto the gravel at the runway's edge as the Chinook is refuelled. I'm now desperate for water. Running over to a group of huts near the runway, I find a group of off-duty Italian aircrew lounging in deckchairs. They're delighted to give me a couple of big bottles of mineral water from a tall fridge behind a home-made bar. I drain them into my camel back, thank them and with a '*Ciao*' dash away, envious of their neat little beards, deep tans and cushy set-up.

After dropping off the Americans at Divisional Headquarters we have a quick de-brief at the Marines' base. No one is too worried about the fact that our mission has been a failure. The Major is still relaxed. I get a thank you. For the assembled NCOs, sweat-stained and weary, it's just another day's work. They're unexcited about the outcome. Perhaps I'm naive but I feel let down by our failure; I hope my next meeting with an Iraqi is less confrontational.

Two days later I'm back in Shai'ba Logistics Base, waiting outside the Commanding Officer's Portakabin. My ultra-short 'high and tight' haircut has not met with his approval. I had it done in an American camp just over the border in Kuwait while coming back from Az Zubayr with the Marines; they have a small guard force there which checks the passports of British Forces personnel crossing the border.

Marching into the office, I come to a formal halt just in

front of the Commanding Officer's desk. The rapid left-right slamming of my heels shakes the entire frame of the flimsy Portakabin.

The CO is displeased. 'The problem, Leo, is that you have shown yourself as wanting to be different to all the other officers . . .'

'God, what bullshit!' I shout inwardly, while nodding contritely. I knew it might cause some mirth among my colleagues but I can't believe that he's bothered by it, given that we're on operations in Iraq, not on parade in London.

'I have no choice but to reflect this in your report as a "lapse of judgement". The adjutant will award you extras.'

'Yes, sir,' I reply, taking my leave with a salute and a sharp turn to my right, slamming my left heel into the floor, again shaking the Portakabin.

'What a load of nonsense,' I think, continuing my unspoken defiance as I walk out into the warm evening. I'm bemused by the fact that in the middle of a counter-insurgency campaign my regiment is under the command of someone who seems more interested in the haircuts of his officers than their operational activity; he didn't even mention the failed arrest operation. Getting 'extras' means I'll have to do extra duties as Picquet Officer – the duty officer – when we're back at our home base in Germany.

The bollocking has touched a nerve because I'm frustrated by the CO's refusal to let me be attached to another unit in Iraq. At the moment I'm often at a loose end because the Scots Guards are in reserve, sitting in Shai'ba Logistics Base. I'm desperate to get out of camp and do something constructive, make some sort of difference, however small. In other regiments – especially those that have a geographical area of responsibility like Basra and Al Amarah – there's plenty going on. Operation Bracken is under way: the Black Watch are up in Babel, in the north, towards the Sunni Triangle, making a show of supporting the US Marine Corps. It's purely political window-dressing in anticipation of the US Presidential election the following month, meant to show the American electorate that the Coalition is rock solid, but it seems exciting. Despite the fact that five Black Watch boys have been blown up by suicide bombs I'd like to go up there. It's the biggest thing going on at the moment for British Forces and we've sent a couple of Scots Guards Captains to be liaison officers. More are required, but ironically because of my Arabic I'm not allowed to go, the CO says, just in case I'm required by him in Shai'ba Logistics Base. I can't help feeling I won't contribute much to the rebuilding of Iraq from here.

To keep me busy the CO takes me as his aide to a series of negotiations between two conflicting tribes in Basra: the Halaf and the Garamsha. In a cold conference room in the Governor of Basra's office we wait by a long table. We've met each side separately already so we're hoping that today they'll agree a truce, mediated by the Tribal Council, a supposedly impartial body of pan-tribal leaders.

The council members, a dozen old men, wander gracefully into the room, resplendent in their flowing *abeyya* gowns (finely spun white or black cloth with broad gold trim, worn over ankle-length *dish-dasha* shirts). Their white-and-black headdresses are kept in place with fat black ropes. Next, the two opposing delegations trickle in and sit down around the long table. The Governor enters and everyone stands, returning his greeting in near unison. He's a handsome forty-something with a neat black beard and smart suit. Supported by the Coalition, he's got the unenviable job of running a city where the electricity supply is more off than on, the police and army are corrupt and a bloody insurgency continues to escalate. He thanks everyone around the table for their attendance and appeals for reconciliation and settlement between the two sides. I get the gist of most of what he says but for the fast bits I strain my ear towards the CO's interpreter.

The Governor leaves soon after his speech. He probably has more important things to do. The mullah, who's from the Iranian-sponsored Supreme Council for Islamic Revolution in Iraq (SCIRI), takes over as chairman when the Governor's tribal-affairs officer, a small man in an ill-fitting suit, fails to get a grip of proceedings.

Both sides make their representations. The Halaf spokesman's resonant voice is accompanied by emphatic hand movements. His anger is sincere but controlled and channelled into frequent rhetorical questions. The Garamsha representative, in an old suit jacket rather than costly *abeyya* gown, is equally passionate but less articulate. His voice reflects the grief of the man sitting next to him – he wears his white headdress without a head-rope as a mark of mourning for his dead son, murdered by the tribal kin of those facing him at the far end of the table.

This death is the latest event in a prolonged feud caused ultimately by the devastation of the marshes. The Garamsha, as marsh dwellers, were deprived of their traditional lifestyle when the vast marshes of Southern Iraq were drained by Saddam after the first Gulf War, in retribution for the failed Shi'a uprising against him. Without water the rich flora and fauna of the marshes' reed beds – which nourished their inhabitants – ceased to exist almost overnight. Destitute, the Garamsha sought refuge in Basra, where the Halaf, as the established tribe, took exception to the sudden incursion of marsh Arab country bumpkins. Both tribes were Shi'a Muslims and had no religious disagreement, but economic competition created animosity and personal feuds, which developed into full-blown tribal conflict involving theft, kidnap and murder. This escalation was fuelled by the unavoidable demands of their tribal code of blood feud, in which blood must be spilled to avenge a death.

After the initial speeches other members of each delegation speak, sometimes at great length. The man whose son has been killed does not speak, but, head bowed, chain-smokes cigarettes. The council members listen while fiddling with prayer beads, talking quietly to one another, answering their phones and snoozing.

The meeting is jolted back to life by a sudden burst of shouting: 'You dog, you have my vehicles!'

'How dare you? You're the thief, unclean bastard!'

Two old men, both of the Garamsha delegation, are chin to chin, gesticulating wildly, their voices rising to incoherent screams. Their peers pull them apart but one breaks free and slaps the face of the other man – who in turn, yelling with blind rage, pulls off his headrope and beats his opponent with it. They enmesh in a thrashing contest before being quickly manhandled apart by members of the Tribal Council.

Sitting apart, the old men look quite feeble, exhausted by their efforts. Breathing hard, they restore their headdresses and wipe specs of saliva from their beards. A few minutes later they're forced to embrace briefly as a formal gesture of reconciliation. I'm thrilled by the sudden burst of activity: they have incredible fire in their bellies for such old men, and though they look spent now, I can't but admire their passionate, ferocious pride.

The excitement seems to reinvigorate the Tribal Council and encourages them, with the mullah's help, to wrap up proceedings. A truce between the two tribes is agreed with a symbolic gesture: the head of each delegation makes a knot in a headdress tied to a walking stick. The mullah announces that the Tribal Council will meet again at a later date to set the amount of blood money to be paid, the crucial element in making the truce last. His words are quickly drowned out as the delegations rise, break into chatter and leave, each side studiously avoiding the other. The members of the Tribal Council are in less of a hurry; after four hours of discussion they continue to converse as the CO and I depart.

Bouncing through Basra in the back of the CO's Snatch (armoured Land-Rover), returning to Shai'ba Logistics Base, I reflect that although the tribal feud is the result of Saddam's draining of the marshes, they're only fighting because the police in Basra are corrupt and ineffectual. Chaos has allowed this tribal violence to escalate, the chaos that filled the vacuum left in Basra after the invasion eighteen months ago. More sinister than the tribal violence is the anti-Coalition insurgency that exploded in the spring. Over the winter it has cooled down but it's bound to kick off again when the weather improves and I'm not sure we're able really to deal with it. We're trying to improve the police and the army but perhaps our very presence is part of the problem and the Iraqis themselves would be better off sorting things out on their own, like they did at the meeting. Our military presence is propping up the local government, but they're almost certainly just as corrupt as anyone else. We're vain if we think we're having a great, morally superior impact.

CHAPTER 2

'What's Arabic for Hello?'

December 2004: Basra, Iraq

It's not long before I meet another tribal sheikh. His house, flat-roofed and low, nestles under a clutch of date palms arching into the clear winter sky. Its white exterior is dulled by a rash of black mould. A rusting footbridge leads over a deep channel of green water and rubbish to the front door. A chorus of croaking toads echoes upwards.

'Welcome,' wheezes the Sheikh, as we enter his reception room in our socks, having stacked our kit inside the door. I'm here because the Sheikh is an ardent supporter of the Coalition and we've got a Scots Guards company doing an operation near his part of town; they're securing the area around a conference centre in Basra where the Iraqi judiciary are deciding on the judicial system for the new Iraq. As the leader of the Basra branch of his tribe the Sheikh is reputed to hold considerable influence over 15,000 subordinate tribesmen. He might be useful in calming any kind of civil disorder we may face. It's my task to be with him for the duration of the operation. I met him yesterday when we devised a plan for him to show me a munitions dump containing explosives that might be used by insurgents.

'Welcome, Captain Loin,' he splutters in English, pleased with his rendition of 'Lion' – the nickname he bestowed on me during yesterday's lunch. 'This house is your house,' he continues, pumping my hand with both of his, a cigarette jammed deep in his fingers.

'This is your house,' he repeats, embracing the man standing next to me.

'Hi, how you doin'?' says Terry, an American officer who's come with me for today's outing.

'What's Arabic for hello?' Terry asks me quietly as we sit down next to our host, pulling our feet under our legs on the thick red carpet. Terry's a Navy Seal Captain who's brought a team up from Kuwait to help with the surveillance of the conference centre. He's interested in seeing a bit of Basra; they've been stuck on their aircraft carrier anchored in the Persian Gulf a great deal lately.

Lowering his chubby frame onto the carpet, the Sheikh beams a broad smile, revealing a small collection of blackish tooth stubs. Wheezing, he ignites a new cigarette from the stub of his old one and inhales deeply. He's clean-shaven and double-chinned under a short moustache and cropped black hair. The bulge of his belly strains the cloth of his black *dish-dasha* shirt, protruding through the open front of a dark suit jacket.

'Abbas!' he roars over his shoulder. A boy's face quickly emerges from a door behind us.

'Bring Bebsi,' the Sheikh instructs, substituting the 'P' unfamiliar to the Arab tongue with a similar sound.

'My eldest son,' he says, turning back to us, beaming again with pride.

18

'It is an honour to be here, O Sheikh,' I say solemnly as cold cans of Pepsi are placed before us.

'This house is your house, a Coalition house,' the Sheikh repeats in automatic obsequy.

The drinks are soon followed by large dishes of rice, roasted chicken, yoghurt and bananas carried in by Abbas, smiling deferentially.

'Abbas!' the Sheikh roars every few moments, sprinkling fragments of masticated rice and chicken. The young boy shuttles back and forth, bringing more food, Pepsi, cigarettes and, finally, tea. The Sheikh answers his mobile repeatedly, barking and wheezing.

I'm happy to allow the Sheikh to think that we have US Special Forces with us especially for his protection, but really they're here because their Unmanned Aerial Vehicle (UAV) – a radio-controlled spy plane – is helping with the surveillance of the conference centre. It's being operated by the rest of Terry's team, who are currently with our company headquarters – a little knot of Warrior armoured vehicles parked up in a muddy field just outside the edge of the city.

After lunch the Sheikh eagerly changes into the set of combats – my own – which I've brought for him, dons my helmet and a radio and climbs into my Snatch wagon, standing up through the hatch in the roof. As we depart, the Sheikh is on top of my vehicle, unrecognised by his own people, guiding us through the streets of suburban Basra. He's delighted and jubilant, as am I, at this mischievous deception.

We head east, out of town and towards the Iranian border. The close-knit dwellings of Basra's outskirts quickly give way to scruffy, rock-strewn desert, interrupted by the sudden green of little irrigated farmsteads. Near a deserted, broken-down farm-dwelling the Sheikh shows us a munitions dump, but it's old debris of the Iran–Iraq war, more than twenty years old. Dozens of mortar rounds, full of explosive, lie in rusty stacks. I mark the location on my GPS (global positioning system); I'll report it later to the intelligence cell. Terry films it with a camcorder.

'These are used by insurgents for making bombs,' says the Sheikh, wheezing.

'You are very kind to show us this place,' I reply. I can't help thinking that the insurgents have probably got much better sources of explosives and wouldn't risk blowing themselves up with this dodgy ordnance. However, it would be churlish to tell the Sheikh this.

I pick up an old helmet. A piece of shrapnel has passed through it, splaying its glass fibres. The inside is dust-ridden, holding no trace of its unfortunate wearer's gore. Nearby, the Sheikh rests cross-legged on a rock and lights up another cigarette.

Returning to town, we take a different route. Near the Sheikh's house we pass rows of small mud dwellings. A power cable above the road catches in the 'cheese-cutter' on my wagon – a defensive bar holding an angled blade to protect the two top-cover guys from electrical cables or maliciously placed wires. The cable falls limply to the road, sliced through.

A man emerges from the house and enquires quietly what we're going to do about it. The Sheikh hides in the vehicle, terrified of his ruse being uncovered.

'We fix it later,' he rasps from behind the wagon door.

I relay this to the man at the side of the road. He accepts it, silently nodding.

The following day the Sheikh is emboldened by the success of his deception, and during lunch is keen to enhance my opinion of his status.

'I have been in Moscow two years ago,' he reveals, eyes glinting. 'For shopping.'

'You are very well travelled, O Sheikh,' I reply with false credulity.

'Also I was invite to Prince Charles' wedding with Camilla . . . I was sorry not to go. He's a good guy.'

I say nothing, silently acknowledging that shameless ego-massaging comes with this sort of territory: I won't burst his bubble. Inwardly, however, I can't help wincing at his desperation to impress. Siding wholeheartedly with the Coalition has raised his status and brought fawning British officers to his door, but in the long term he may have backed the wrong horse. As he waves me farewell I ponder what will become of him when the Coalition withdraws.

Back in camp, I'm called to see the CO. He's been sorting out officers' jobs for the coming year.

'When we get back to Germany, Leo,' he says, unsmiling, 'you're to be the Intelligence Officer.' This is not what I'd been expecting; we previously agreed that I'd go on the long Arabic course after the tour and eventually return to Iraq as a proper interpreter.

'What about the Arabic, sir?' I ask, trying to be upbeat. 'I was expecting to continue . . .'

'Well, you can do, you'll just have to wait a bit,' he replies, frowning.

This is bad news; it means at least eighteen months back in Germany doing repetitive, tedious training exercises without, crucially, any operational tours. The prospect is terrifyingly dull and, having started the Arabic, it's the last place I want to be. Perhaps I'd be better off leaving and doing my own thing? I could travel for a year and learn Arabic on my own, and maybe go back to Damascus. I didn't join the Army to waste my youth training in Germany, and having waited so long for this tour I really don't like being told to 'wait a bit' again.

The good news, however, is that I'm allowed to join a Scots Guards company that has deployed to Maysan Province, far to the north of Basra. It's a desolate place of muddy plains and salt flats interrupted by oil pipelines, smoking stacks of brick kilns, clumps of date palms and ramshackle pylon lines.

On 30 January 2005 I'm in an operations room in Maymunah, a small town north of Al Amarah, Maysan Province's volatile capital. I'm with a platoon securing the police station during the first national elections of the new Iraq. We're supposed to be discreet, to allow the whole process to be presented as Iraqi-led, but our Warrior Armoured Fighting Vehicles (AFVs) are parked menacingly outside the front gate, surrounded by barbed wire. We give the police some credibility. In our absence they're ineffective due to corruption; poorly paid, they're susceptible to bribes, and their loyalty is multi-faceted to an extent that we can only begin to fathom.

It's a pleasure to get away from the mud and stinking Portaloos of camp. The police station is a solid flat-roofed building which encloses a large grubby courtyard bustling with blue-shirted policemen. They tout Kalashnikovs and shout into walkie-talkies. I'm on the radio most of the time, speaking to another team in a neighbouring town. I share the operations room with a police Major, the district and station commander.

He's an engaging man, with striking black-lined eyes, a swarthy face pitted with pox scars, and an untidy moustache. He wears a sports sweater under his blue shirt against the biting cold. A subordinate Iraqi policeman listens to their radio – an American HF system – and simultaneously watches TV: Hollywood violence under flickering Arabic subtitles.

The Major shares his lunch with me – delicious kebabs of mutton still hot from the roadside stall. Picking up bits of meat with flat bread, we munch away, adding onion segments and nibbling slender green chillies with each mouthful.

'The Shi'a list will win,' he replies in answer to my question about the election. His answer is unsurprising, given the poster advocating the main Shi'a party on the wall outside.

'But of course most Sunnis cannot vote,' he whispers with a chuckle, sharing the humour with the radio operator.

'They will stay in their homes, it is too dangerous to go outside,' he says, referring to the Sunni Triangle far to our north, where the level of violence is much higher than here in the Shi'a heartland of southern Iraq. This fact, combined with fears of political domination by the Shi'a majority, has led some elements of the formerly powerful Sunni minority to boycott the election, hoping that a reduced Sunni participation might discredit the results and stall the Shi'a ascendancy.

Having lost political clout with the fall of Saddam, the Sunni minority are not only terrified of this political role-reversal but concerned also about their loss of control over the vast oil reserves that lie in the Shi'a south and Kurdish north; the Sunni lands of central Iraq hold none.

The Major's words are an ominous glimpse of the sectarian schism hanging over Iraq.

'Insh'allah here it will pass peacefully,' he says with a raised finger, encouraging me to share his prognosis.

His hand comes to rest conspicuously on the Glock pistol in a shiny brown leather holster on his hip – a prize possession and status guarantor supplied by the Coalition, and in consequence repeatedly asked for by all policemen and army officers.

From the police station's roof I can see the election in full swing. Voters wait in a ragged line to be searched before entering the polling station, a blue-painted school across the street. The women are searched by other veiled females behind a white hospital screen. Explanatory posters adorn the walls; a colourful cartoon flow chart starts with a ballot box and leads to three other stages, which my eyes cannot distinguish. The atmosphere is peaceful and almost festive.

Two police guards emerge from their watchtower, and join me in silently watching the polling station.

'Good,' I say, pointing towards the voters below.

'Good, very good,' replies one of them in English. Proudly, they both hold up ink-stained finger tips: they've voted.

It's a pleasing moment: democracy visibly in action in Iraq for the first time in half a century. But as my gaze moves from their blue-black fingertips to our Warrior AFVs at the police station's front gate, the illusion is abruptly punctured. The election is a fragile and almost false construct, well-meaning but self-defeating in its dependence on the presence of British troops and heavy armour.

Before coming to Iraq I dismissed the false basis for invasion. None of us in the Scots Guards officers' mess believed the Weapons of Mass Destruction nonsense; we knew it was a pretext for the toppling of a dictator, which surely must be good news. My overriding emotion was a desire to be there – this at last was action! After a long and arduous professional training, my desire to actually get involved in something real, dangerous and uncertain was overwhelming.

Up on this rooftop, however, I'm feeling a bit uneasy. The pseudo-democracy happening before our eyes surely doesn't justify the chaos and trauma that our invasion and occupation have brought to Iraq.

Descending from the roof, I realise that I'm sick of seeing Iraq from inside barbed-wire compounds, from armoured rooftops, from the turret of a Warrior. Even, simply, from inside a uniform.

From Maysan Province I'm called back to Shai'ba Logistics Base. I'm to be the second-in-command for one of the battalion's rifle companies. We're on constant standby to deploy into Basra at the behest of the brigade commander and arrest suspect individuals.

At about 2300 I'm woken by a call from the company commander:

'Crash the boys out in Snatch – there's something on.'

I wake Scotty, one of the platoon commanders, who shares my tent.

'We're going out . . . Stand to and get ready in Snatch.'

He dashes off to alert the other two platoon commanders and then his platoon sergeant. I jump onto my bicycle and burn round to the CSM's tent.

'We're on . . . I'm going over to the ops room.'

'Aye, nae bother, sir,' he replies in his confident Inverness-shire tone, promptly emerging from his mosquito net.

Peddling frantically, I head over to the operations room among the white-box cluster of Portakabins. I'm going there to get a brief from the company commander – all the stuff he can't tell me on the mobile phone:

'Right, Leo,' he says in an urgent whisper. 'We're going into Basra to help two-two grab a high-value target.' His eyes are wide with excitement: 'two-two' means the 22 SAS Regiment. Getting out our 'spot maps' of central Basra he marks where we're going: 'The target house is here . . . Seven Platoon will be the lead group with the blades [SAS soldiers] who'll blow the doors and identify the bravo [male target] . . . I'll be just behind Seven Platoon. Nine Platoon will be the inner cordon here with you, Eight Platoon will be the outer cordon here,' he says, drawing two concentric rings around the black pin-prick that marks the target house.

'Get the company here asap. The two-two blokes will brief us in detail before we go.'

I scream back to the company's line of tents to find everyone now frantically preparing, packing themselves and their kit into the wagons amid the dust-laden glare of headlights.

'This is gleaming,' I think. A huge jolt of electricity has been sent through the company; everyone's up for it.

A couple of minutes later the six commanders – three sergeants and three young platoon commanders – and the CSM are around me. Their bodies are cluttered with body armour, webbing vests and rifles, and trailing radio headsets. They're wearing head-torches and clutch their maps intently. I relay the outline plan with the help of a scrawled whiteboard sketch balanced on my vehicle bonnet. The commanders are deliberately calm, determined not to show any hint of excitement on behalf of the SAS.

Mounting up into our Snatch wagons, each team reports ready to me. We rattle over to the operations room. Lined up behind me are a dozen Snatch vehicles in column. It's been less than half an hour since the call so we've done well, it's been a fast crash-out. Calling the team commanders together, we go in to the Battalion Headquarters. Jammed into a tiny Portakabin, we crowd around a desk under a humming strip light.

Bob, the SAS bloke who's done the reconnaissance, takes us through the plan:

'I'm not teaching you guys to suck eggs but I'll run through it just so we're all happy . . . Once the outer cordon is in place the lead group will dismount with me and move forward here.' He points on the map to a street running north towards the objective. 'If I could ask you to put one team on either side of the road that'll allow you to cover the rooftops of the houses on the opposite side of the road.'

Pointing to a black-and-white satellite photograph, he shows us the target house, a substantial flat-roofed building surrounded by a wall.

'I'll lead the break-in team to the front door and Kiwi'll blow 'em in.'

Kiwi, a rangy SAS bloke with a buck-toothed grin, nods. 'I'll make a bit of a bang on the door and might have to use the twelve-gauge if it stays on its hinges,' he says, dangling a black pump-action shotgun under his arm.

Bob continues: 'When we're in you can do your bit – you know how. But get everyone down asap, I'll have a look to ID 'em. When you're searching, show everything to me. I speak the lingo. On the way out, if we get any bother we'll get the top cover (helicopter support) down to give us a bit of rat-ta-ta-tatt.'

Wiry and slight, with a neat brown beard (he's trimmed it and clean-shaved his cheeks in the smart, typically Iraqi fashion) and clear blue eyes, Bob strikes me as intensely able and unforgiving. He's wearing a standard-issue set of chest webbing but his green (not desert) combat jacket and civilian walking boots make him, in contrast to us, exotic and intriguing. As we leave the room, he chats to his colleague Kevin. Stocky, with a dyed-black beard, a hint of ginger in his eyebrows and hair that is too black against his fair skin, his chest is festooned with green canvas ammunition pouches.

None of the three wears rank but I can tell from their age and demeanour that they're senior NCOs, probably staff sergeants or warrant officers. They're a breath of utterly exciting fresh air, a wonderful contrast to the grim orthodoxy of the Scots Guards. The staff officers in the headquarters who aren't deploying onto the ground sniff slightly, trying to show they really aren't impressed, they've seen this all before – which of course they haven't.

At 0100 we race into Basra. The streets are deserted. The moonlight reflects off the brimming roadside gutters. The target house is in an upmarket part of town: the streets are broad and the roads properly paved with tarmac. On either side of us high-walled compounds, with the upper boughs of trees spilling over, screen large houses.

Bringing up the rear of the convoy, I've got Corporal Montgomery driving and a couple of signallers in the back. We glide to a halt on the right-hand side of the road, as described in our orders. The lead team and company commander's group are ahead of us. Their shadowy figures emerge to the right of their wagons, making a hurried, hushed dismount.

They disappear off to our right in a tightly packed caterpillar huddle. I pass all the empty wagons and stop at the corner of a street branching away to the right. The target house is down there somewhere on the right-hand side. Left with my team, I send Monty to turn around some of the wagons left without drivers, so they're all facing the right way for our extraction. I also put one of the top-cover blokes at the corner to keep an eye on the target, and leave the other on top of the wagon. I stand next to my door, near the radio, although we're on radio silence until the break-in team enter the house.

The night is silent. My mental picture of the break-in team creeping towards the front door is interrupted as *bumph!* – a huge explosive thud shatters the air, seemingly much closer than it is. A ripple of dog-barking spreads around us. The radio crackles into life as the company commander's signaller starts relaying events back to headquarters: 'First team

29

inside . . . We're inside . . . Two bravoes, one echo . . . We're searching.'

I listen in; this means that they've found two men and a woman.

Out of a door in the compound wall beside us, two faces peer timorously. I greet them. A man in his twenties, with a short moustache and yellow tracksuit, steps cautiously out of the door.

'Why the explosion?' he asks, smiling nervously, with an inquisitory inwards spin-flick of the opened fingers typical to Iraqis.

'We're arresting terrorists,' I reply solemnly, glad that my answer carries weight.

'Good, very good.' He speaks in English, accompanied by a raised thumb. 'God be with you,' he says, slipping back into his compound and closing the metal door.

The company commander comes up on the radio. 'We're coming out with one echo.' So the detainee is female.

I send two wagons round the corner and warn the helicopter that's circling unheard above us that we're about to extract to the pick-up point. The convoy, simultaneously starting engines, roars into life. A brief flurry of excitement flickers through my stomach.

The pair of wagons shortly re-emerges, wobbling with top-heaviness, chased by the break-in team scurrying along, their faces shiny with streams of sweat, wide-eyed and jubilant. They jump into their wagons with breathless, whispered instructions.

We get a 'follow on' from the company commander over the radio as our convoy grinds forward, going back the way we came. At a large junction the teams providing the inner and outer cordons arrive simultaneously to rejoin us; this is good timing. I count all the wagons in, telling the company commander over the radio:

'We're all in – good to go.'

We zoom south out of the city, triumphant at our success and exhilarated by the sudden speed.

In the city's outskirts we pull up by the roadside. A Chinook comes down on a patch of wasteland, to the bewilderment of the few passing drivers. A cluster of bodies scuttles across towards it; it's the SAS guys bundling away the prisoner. They disappear up the tailgate, and the Chinook rises up and vanishes noisily into the black sky.

Back in my tent with Scotty, it's past dawn before we sleep. He commanded the break-in team and is still wired with excitement.

'It was a bird . . . Behind a brick wall on the stairs. Said she was a judge, can you believe it? They ID'd her and took a load of documents. Man, that was fucking gleaming!'

Forty-eight hours later, we're told something's wrong. The company commander is summoned to headquarters. He calls me:

'This is direct from the CO. Go and get a load of white paint from the Quartermaster. It turns out that the echo we grabbed really *was* a High Court Judge . . . The brigade commander's making an apology to the Governor and we're on stand-by to fix the door and repaint her house.'

'You're fucking joking!' I blurt back, the laughter rising in my voice.

'No, I'm deadly serious,' he replies. 'Anyway, the company

did a bloody good job, so it's a success from our point of view.'

Returning from the Quartermaster, I stack four six-gallon tins of white paint and a load of brushes in my tent and wonder who cocked up. Was it the SAS? Was it higher up, whoever feeds them their intelligence? Perhaps it was the right person and she's just exploiting her position to be released. I simply don't know.

Soon afterwards I submit a letter resigning my commission to the CO. I'm disillusioned and frustrated. If I stay in the Army, I'll be stuck in the tedious rut of regimental life for more than a year, after which the best chance of excitement will be coming back out to Iraq. I've come to realise over the past few months that our presence here is at best misguided and clumsy, at worst deceptive and immoral.

I've been struggling reluctantly to work it out. I know the Weapons of Mass Destruction issue was a pretext, but if we came here to replace a brutal dictator with democracy then we're making a terrible hash of it. The facade of democracy we've created doesn't justify the chaos and sectarian bloodshed unleashed by our invasion and unresolved by our continued occupation.

I've got an unpleasant feeling that ultimately, behind the layers of pretext, we're here because of the oil in the ground beneath us, in a botched attempt to secure a dependable supply to fuel our economy. I dismissed as left-wing nonsense the 'no blood for oil' rhetoric that appeared in much of the press during the time of the invasion but now I'm not so sure. Oil infrastructure is ever-present throughout Basra and

Maysan Provinces. Wire-fenced refineries house vast tangles of metal piping. Flare pipes spew out great plumes of orange flame, burning the by-product gas that's uneconomic to bottle. Dirty pipelines criss-cross the desert. It's all part of Iraq's scenery, ubiquitous and hardly noticed, yet if it wasn't here, would we be?

I'm disillusioned, but at the same time I'm not angry – I simply don't want to face it. There are nearly 10,000 British troops here just getting on with the job, taking terrible risks and dying for the sake of a doomed project, and yet *crack on* they do, like it's inevitable, reasonable and sensible to be here. The error of our presence in Iraq is so fundamental, so enormous that it's invisible, beyond analysis, and best avoided. I just want to break free from the crushing futility of serving here to explore the Middle East and Asia on my own terms.

My resignation is accepted without hesitation, as is normal in the Scots Guards; there's no shortage of new officers keen to join this ancient and prestigious regiment.

The last weeks in Iraq drag slowly past. We're on constant standby, ready for more nocturnal arrests, but the call never comes.

My tent-mate's collection of paperbacks is a welcome diversion. Rummaging in his trunk I find a book written by a Victorian member of the Household Division: *A Ride to Khiva* by Captain Fred Burnaby. It's a compelling account of a journey made in 1875 through Imperial Russia to the last independent Central Asian Khanate, now in Uzbekistan. Burnaby was obsessed by the extent to which the Czar's influence had advanced towards British India. This issue was at the core of the Great Game, the covert and intrigue-filled struggle between the Russian and British empires for dominance of the remote yet strategically invaluable parts of Central Asia just beyond their borders. Thirsting for adventure and without the sanction of his superiors, Burnaby set off during his winter leave to play the Great Game for all he was worth. Racing through the pages of antiquated typescript, my imagination is fired. It seems that, like Burnaby, my surest route to adventure is to do my own thing. I crave the limitless freedom of travelling alone, beholden to nobody. The ridiculous paradox is that I'm *leaving* the Army to pursue excitement abroad. Counting down the last turgid days before quitting our sterile camp, I give my imagination free rein; it takes me east, riding through central Asia. I make daydream plans to retrace Burnaby's journey on my departure from the Army.

Before this, however, I must do my time; I still have one year to serve according to the terms of my engagement. It seems I might avoid the extra duties awarded for my incongruous haircut as I'm to be posted, after our return from Iraq, to our ceremonial company in London.

CHAPTER 3

'Nothing like Iraq'

August 2005: London

Facing forward, but glancing right, I draw breath. The column of marching Guardsmen, their scarlet tunics shaded by my black bearskin fringe, wheels to the left.

'Buckingham Palace detachment,' I roar, watching the column move past, right to left. The regimental colour flag, carried at the head of the column, draws opposite. This is my cue:

'Pre-seeeeent arms!'

Three palm-slapping cracks ring out in unison as the dozen Guardsmen behind me strike their weapons into a position of symbolic deference, held out to the front, bayonets uppermost. Simultaneously I move my sword upwards, pressing the hilt to my chin, and then down to my right side, tucked in behind my thigh, the shiny blade tip hovering just above the forecourt's red gravel. I stand stock-still. I'm sweating profusely into my thick tunic, still faithful to a centuries-old pattern designed to deflect musket-balls. It's made even heavier by the gold cuffs and collar, with silver sequins fashioned into a thistle, my regimental emblem. My thick woollen trousers – blue with fat red stripes down the sides of the legs – further insulate me, sending rivulets of sweat trickling down my shins and into my boots.

The column disappears through the forecourt's heavy ornamental gates, heading for the Mall.

'Slooooope arms!' I roar again, stretching and bellowing the order. I return my sword to its position of carriage: held out to my front, the blade vertical. Turning about, I see the Guardsmen in three ranks before me. I position myself at their head and we march over to the guardroom at the side of the Palace, accompanied only by the rhythmic crunching of our heels on the gravel.

Entering the guardroom, I breathe a sigh of relief. That's another Guard mount done, or 'Changing of the Guard' as it's commonly known. I'm commanding the Buckingham Palace half of the new Guard, who'll stand outside the palace for the next twenty-four hours. The column that's just marched down the Mall will provide the Guard at St James's Palace, the London home of Prince Charles and his sons.

Leaving the Palace forecourt I wander through the park to St James's, or *Jimmy's* as we know it. I'm plagued by a throng of tourists taking turns to trot excitedly alongside me and snap one another's photograph. I've now been back in London for a month doing 'public duties'. My morale is high. I'm delighted to be here. I've got bags of time off in between Guards to really get about town, ride out in Hyde Park, see my friends and prepare for life after the Army. I'm also very excited about the prospect of five weeks of summer leave starting in a couple of days.

I walk into the Queen's Guard mess, where the table, set for a large lunch, is laden with gleaming silver, countless crystal glasses and immaculate napkins. The room is encrusted with military oil paintings, ornamental silver, walnut furniture and chandeliers. I feel deep in the womb of martial privilege. At the gilded epicentre of the establishment, this really is the last untouched bastion of the old-school Army. There are two other officers on Guard with me and we'll stay here for the next two days. We can have guests up to dine but, finding long dinners tedious, I have guests infrequently, and focus more on doing long runs around the parks.

Public duties are fun while being purely superficial. We're here to look good, to represent the majesty of the Queen. The security of the Royal palaces depends on the high-tech monitoring of the Metropolitan Police, not the Guardsmen on sentry. The officers, whose social lives tend to thrive in London, generally have an absolute hoot, but for the young Guardsmen it's tedious; they're prone to becoming fat and poor while drinking away their wages in the city's fleshpots.

Coming off Guard, we finish the parade in Wellington Barracks, where I live. In my rooms on the third floor – which overlook Buckingham Palace and St James's park – I pull off my tunic with the help of Lambe, my orderly, a biddable eighteen-year-old from Lanarkshire with orange hair and spectacles. I've appointed him because he's keen to learn and seems loyal. His predecessor, an excellent orderly, is now doing time in Colchester Military Correction Centre prior to being discharged from the Army for absence without leave; he was gone for almost three years, during which time he was an unsuccessful landscape gardener.

Putting on a suit, I take the Tube – a form of transport officially deemed beneath the dignity of a Foot Guards officer, but these Standing Orders are sensibly ignored – to Sloane Square. Emerging, I stroll down to Chelsea Barracks, a mishmash of near-derelict 1960s architecture. I'm told the architect defrauded the MoD, went to jail and was a suicide. Perhaps he felt remorse for the state of the Guardsmen's accommodation: the damp, cramped four-man rooms are a travesty. Nothing's done about it because the Barracks have been on the verge of demolition for the last decade. There's a plan afoot now to sell the entire site.

I meet one of my fellow platoon commanders. He's been recently bruised by a scandalous encounter with a pair of hookers: he stupidly brought them into Wellington Barracks and, as a result of their camera phones, ended up with his face splashed across the *Sun* newspaper, to much regimental outrage and secret mirth. He needs cheering up, so, with him explaining his side of the story, we wander down the King's Road to find lunch.

A month later I'm wearing a grimy knee-length shirt and baggy trousers (*shalwar qamiz*), an itchy woollen flat hat and a cheap cotton scarf. I've got a short scruffy beard, and am utterly thrilled to be in Afghanistan.

Indulging my passionate interest in Pakistan and its Urdu language, I spent the early weeks of my leave riding and playing rustic polo in a village beyond Chitral, high in the remote and mountainous Northern Areas of Pakistan. Returning towards Islamabad, I paused in Peshawar, and couldn't resist the temptation to dash through the Khyber Pass to Kabul and onwards to the Panjshir valley.

I've been completely drawn in by the intoxicating brand

of heroism and danger that the North Western Frontier Province and Afghanistan represent. I'm as far from London as I possibly can be in every sense and loving it.

In front of me stands a green-domed and whitewashed mausoleum, the tomb of Ahmed Shah Masood, the iconic former leader of the Northern Alliance Mujahideen. Intriguing and charismatic, Commander Masood, as he's called in Afghanistan, was the Taliban's most bitter and enduring enemy. With his fellow Tajiks, he held out in the Panjshir valley, where I stand now, which never fell to the Taliban. The Northern Alliance, allied with the US-led Coalition, eventually swept the Taliban from power in the wake of 9/11. But it did so without Masood: he was murdered by Al Qaeda suicide bombers just three days before September 11. The bombers, posing as Moroccan television journalists, were sent by Osama Bin Laden as a means of repaying his Taliban host's hospitality. Since his expulsion from Sudan in the late nineties, Bin Laden had based himself in Afghanistan as a guest and benefactor of his fellow Sunni fundamentalists.

Inside the mausoleum a marble slab lies flat, hidden by a green velvet cover richly embroidered with Qur'anic verses in silver and gold. A Mujahid in camouflage trousers sits unarmed and cross-legged at the side, his flat woollen pakol cap worn at the very back of his head in the unmistakeable style of his dead leader.

Hesitantly, I pull out my camera. The pair of young men who've brought me here in their car smile delightedly: it seems that photographing the grave will honour it. Leaving the mausoleum, I want to ask them about their lives, about the Panjshir valley and Masood. But I know neither Dari nor

Tajik, and they speak only a few words of Urdu. In silence we move to a little wooden kiosk, the only other building in the mausoleum's vicinity. It's selling Masood paraphernalia, and I choose a poster with his smiling face set under the inscription 'The Martyr and Mujahid Commander Ahmed Shah Masood'. Resigned to it being squashed, I slide it into my dusty satchel.

Beside the shack lies a derelict Sherman tank. I can't imagine what bizarre route this particular piece of hardware, of American manufacture during the Second World War, took to its final resting place. Almost all of the ubiquitous defunct war materiel littering the valley is of Soviet origin. Armoured hulks are often adapted as components in domestic construction or lie half-covered by dust, claimed by the barren earth as part of the landscape.

Returning to the nearest village, Rokha, just five kilometres from the tomb, I'm approached by the local policeman, who beckons me into a chair on the police station's veranda. Surrounded by a knot of curious villagers, he scrutinises my passport, for much of the time upside-down. Surrounded by villagers in *shalwar qamiz*, he seems more incongruous than I, in his khaki uniform and outsized Soviet cap – looking like a fancy-dress parody, a fat grimy meringue. After an hour of repeated assurances that I'm an Australian student, the policeman is content. The fact that, as a serving British Army officer, I'm forbidden to be in Afghanistan unofficially during my leave makes this minor deception entertaining rather than nerve-racking. I'm not fearful; I trust their hospitality and am convinced that my trust will be reciprocated. The policeman shakes my hand and directs me to a shared cab, in which I can head back down the valley towards Kabul.

The road hugs the valley side, high above the blue-green torrent of the Panjshir river. The valley sides themselves are of dry earth disturbed by a shock of verdure at the water's edge. Stopping off at a roadside eating-house, we piss behind its concrete walls and wash our hands and faces. Inside, we tuck into plates of Uzbeki pilau – a mound of steaming rice, cooked with ghee, raisins, shards of carrot and almonds, piled over a fatty lump of mutton. Imitating the cab driver's actions, I compact a little ball of hot rice with the fingertips of my right hand and flick it into my mouth. It's delicious. A poster of Masood, similar to the one I've just bought, watches over us. There's also a rug woven in his image hanging by the cashier's wooden table. One of my co-travellers pays for my lunch, and while refusing repayment mentions a Dari word I do know: '*mehman*', meaning 'guest'.

Out of the valley, closer to Kabul, we're passed by a column of Dutch armoured vehicles heading for the nearby Bagram Air Base. A pair of Black Hawk helicopters zip past, scanning the road ahead of another convoy which soon thunders past. It's made up of huge trucks packed with dusty soldiers, their faces hidden by helmets and goggles. A 'SEMPER FI' ('always faithful') sticker on a door reveals they're US Marines.

A veterinary doctor who we've picked up at Charikar, a small town at the mouth of the valley, shares the front passenger seat with me. He's astonished by my presence.

'It's too dangerous for you. Why are you here?' he asks in English.

'To see Afghanistan,' I reply, secretly amused at his reaction.

'Do not travel at night, and if you have any problem, call me; here is my number.'

Folding the small square of paper, I thank him sincerely, touched by his kindness.

Back in Kabul I stroll about with perfect ease; it's such an ethnic and sartorial hotchpotch that I'm not out of place. Fair hair and blue eyes are not uncommon, and my clothes are local. I'm stopped by a man with a laden cart, asking me to read an address for him. Though familiar with the Persian script, I can't decipher the scrawl; and not knowing Dari, Kabul's predominant language, I hand it back with a shrug of my shoulders, silently claiming illiteracy.

This is thrilling! I'm delighted that I'm generally taken as Afghan until I speak, when my bad Urdu exposes me as a Chitrali perhaps, from northern Pakistan. I love the deceptive mischief involved in playing this role. But more, I love the sensation of seeing things without them being altered by my presence; it's the absolute reverse of experiencing Iraq in a uniform.

At a roadside juice stall I drink cold, sweet mango pulp. Having become a frequent customer in the last couple of days, I'm greeted by Hamood the Pashtun stall owner. He's keen to express his preference for the Afghan parliamentary elections, due next month.

'I will not vote for anyone with a beard: the Mujahideen killed my father and my two brothers. Dr Najibullah [the Soviet puppet premier brutally murdered by the Taliban on their capture of Kabul in 1996] was the best president,' he says in Urdu.

'How's business? It's good, since the end of the Taliban ...'

In the busy traffic, a black Land Cruiser with opaque windows pulls up, escorted by a beige US Army Humvee. Dismounting, a couple of soldiers in unusual greyish cam-ouflage walk up the street. One of them walks right past me; he's wearing a helmet and sunglasses, with his rifle slung to his side. An eagle's-head badge is Velcroed to his left arm. He looks bizarre and fairly lethal but also vulnerably incongru-ous. Watching him sideways, I finish my juice, silently tri-umphant at going unnoticed in an Afghan crowd.

Leaving the stall, I reflect again on the strand of interest that brought me here in the first place: learning Urdu in Lahore, before joining the Army. I relished the cultural sub-mersion involved in throwing myself, anonymous and hum-ble, into a society: adopting its dress, eating its food, and striving to learn its poetic and beautiful language. I was drenched, drawn in, intoxicated by the culture and hospital-ity of those around me.

Now, here in Afghanistan, this passion has returned, more strongly. I feel a glorious sensation of being in the thick of it, absorbed, alert, all excess concerns stripped away. I've attained a simplicity of form and intent which allows a greater appreci-ation of my surroundings. I'm in awe of these people who, often despite terrible poverty, still live their lives by social tenets of honour and hospitality, long forgotten by my own society. I feel privileged to have received their generosity, and each successful conversation in Urdu gives me a surge of joy.

But my Urdu is imperfect and I know neither Dari nor Pashtu. The satisfaction is fleeting. I want to get closer to the Afghans, to live absolutely on their terms. I'm gripped by a desire not only to pass through a crowd of Afghans un-noticed, like a latter-day Great Gamer, but to be able to participate and engage with them in their own language. I know that I must return.

Back in London, I'm clean-shaven and in a greatcoat. Public duties continue in winter order. I've got another few months to do before my departure from the Army in the spring. On Queen's Guard, I unfold my map of Asia on the billiard table. I'm planning to retrace Burnaby's ride to Khiva, and then keep going. With growing excitement, I study place names along his route from Russia to Central Asia: St Petersburg, Moscow, Orenburg, the Aral Sea and Khiva. From there I want to go even further: on to Bokhara, Samarqand and Afghanistan.

My finger comes to a halt at Peshawar; my memories of this chaotic Pashtun frontier town at the foot of the Khyber Pass are still fresh from my autumn travels. On returning through the Pass to Peshawar, I saw its university, a splendid red sandstone monument of Imperial gothic-orientalism. Why not go to Peshawar to study Pashtu? Guardsman Lambe's arrival jolts me back to current reality; I must prepare for the guard dismount.

Later, in Wellington Barracks, I get a call from James, a Scots Guards contemporary.

'I've just spoken to the Adjutant [officer in charge of discipline and manning] at 3 Para. They're after Captains who've got their wings to go on Operation Herrick, to Afghanistan . . . I know you're leaving but just thought it might interest you.'

He's right. My interest *is* pricked. A phone call to a friend in 3 Para reveals that they've been 'warned off' to deploy in the spring to Helmand Province, in the lawless, opium-growing south of Afghanistan, as part of a big counter-narcotics and 'nation-building' effort. They need a Captain to act as a company second-in-command. Having passed the 'P Coy' pre-parachute selection and the 'Jumps' course, I've got my Para 'wings' and I'm therefore qualified to serve with a Para battalion. Tantalisingly, there are Army Pashtu courses being run specifically for the deployment.

Before I speak to the 3 Para Adjutant, it occurs to me that my experience of travelling in that region and my knowledge of Urdu would perhaps make me more useful outside a battalion; and in any case I've already experienced the frustration of being tied to my own unit in Iraq. Surely I could do the Pashtu course and go along as some sort of liaison officer? There's been a minor British presence in Afghanistan since 2001, with troops in Kabul as part of the International Security Assistance Force (ISAF), and in the northern city of Mazar-e-Sharif as a 'Provincial Reconstruction Team', but this big deployment to Helmand is a new operation. Despite not knowing any details, I'm drawn to the idea of going to the Pashtun south of Afghanistan and intrigued by the intent: 'nation-building' sounds fascinating and very honourable. I imagine myself speaking Pashtu and cutting deals with Pashtun tribal elders while drinking tea in the Hindu Kush. What an awesome prospect! It's exactly the sort of experience I'm leaving the Army to pursue. Ironically it seems that, on the verge of my leaving the Army, the ideal opportunity to play a new version of the Great Game has presented itself. Perhaps I should stay for a bit longer?

Another phone call to the headquarters of 16 Air Assault Brigade, the unit deploying, is conclusive.

'I'm being posted to 3 Para,' I say to the Chief of Staff, using a white lie. 'But I thought as I've been around that part of the world and speak a bit of the lingo that I might be more use to you as a liaison officer . . . Getting involved with the local population is what I love,' I say, eagerly recounting my previous travels, including my illegal foray into Afghanistan.

'I think we might have something for you . . . Do you speak Pashtu?'

'No, but I'll get myself on the course, so I'll be ready by March,' I reply, the decision to stay having flashed through my head – unthinking, automatic almost.

'OK, you're onboard. See you then.'

That's it! I'm staying in and going to Afghanistan! This is amazing! I can't believe that a senior officer can be so positive and decisive. Hurriedly picking up the phone again, I book myself on the Pashtu course. Another phone call to the Army manning department in Glasgow reverses my resignation. It's immediate, because it's for operational reasons. I'm thrilled by the executive urgency of all of this; it's so unlike the stulti-fying protocol and negativity that smothers enthusiasm in the regiment. Luckily, this should make it past the Scots Guards Adjutant: only when the official posting order gets faxed from Glasgow to 16 Air Assault Brigade and copied to the Scots Guards will he find out, and faced with an officially sanctioned fait accompli, be powerless to change it.

At the Cenotaph a few days later, I'm at the head of a detach-ment of Guardsmen at the Remembrance ceremony. Standing still, in bearskin and greatcoat with my sword resting tip-down on the road, I strain to see any movement from Downing Street: our cue to brace up. Around the sandstone memorial thick ranks of soldiers, sailors and airmen are drawn up. The band plays soft contemplative music as we wait for the wreath-laying to begin. I've got woollen skiing socks on but I can feel the cold of Whitehall's tarmac through my boot soles. I had a drop of port before coming out but that was three hours ago. Anyway, I wouldn't dare complain about the cold or the tedium of standing still for three hours when our purpose is to commemorate the dead and honour the surviving veterans of all wars.

Standing unmoving, I reflect on my recent change of plan. Though I've nothing more than a general idea of what I might be doing, I'm completely certain it'll be interesting. I feel lucky to be going; the couple of friends that I've told about it in confidence, still serving in the battalion, are out-raged with jealousy.

'You jammy sod!' cried Scotty down the phone line from Germany. He knew what I was talking about because the deployment hit the headlines last week: 'I read about it today, sounds like the wild west!'

'I know. The locals call it the Desert of Death.' I chuckled, entertained by the comic gloominess of the name. Like Scotty, I'd also read that morning's papers and seen the 'Dasht-e-Margo', as it's known in the Persian vernacular, sweeping across Afghanistan's southern border, covering an area greater than Wales and swallowing the bottom half of Helmand Province.

*

Poring over the increasing press coverage, I'm increasingly thrilled at my coming involvement in an important cutting-edge project. I'm mustard keen on the idea of 'nation-building' and getting really involved with the Afghans. I consume as much background information as I can on the region.

I attend a lecture in the cosy library of the Royal Society for Asian Affairs, where a noted scholar and Afghan expert narrates, to much amusement, chunks of an Imperial mem-sahib's diary. Full of dry wit and stoicism, it relates the dreadful hardships and tragedies of the British retreat from Kabul towards Jalalabad in 1842. As I listen I'm grateful that we won't make such foolish errors this time around. Indeed, it reinforces my secret self-image as a new Great Game player, serving NATO, not the Empire.

At the fringe of the suited, mostly geriatric audience sits a girl with a strikingly elegant neck and dark skin. She's been living in Kazakhstan, she tells me after the lecture. She's nearly as tall as my 6 feet 4 inches, with brown eyes that flash when she emphasises her words. Intrigued, I ask for her card, determined to get in touch and e-mail her some queries I have about riding in that part of the world.

My last Guard is in December at Windsor Castle. It involves a mini Changing of the Guard, followed by two glorious days spent visiting the Guardsmen on 'stag' (standing on sentry), running in the Great Park, and relaxing in the perfect solitude of the officer's flat. Its ancient oak panelling bears the epigrams, sketches, names and initials of the countless Guards officers who've captained the Guard and entertained in the flat over the last two hundred years.

Having enjoyed a festive evensong in the chapel, I despatch Guardsman Lambe to get a box of mince pies from the high street. The girl I met at the lecture is coming to tea.

'Are your boots made of plastic?' asks Lucy, picking up one of my gleaming black Wellingtons.

'No,' I reply, quickly taking it from her to avoid more fingerprints, 'but Guardsman Lambe is a bulling genius.'

Like a boot alchemist, Guardsman Lambe can change dull leather to reflective glass, 'bulling' the leather with beeswax and polish.

Replacing the boot with a mince pie, I listen with increasing fascination as she recounts her travels: an epic nine-month journey along the ancient Silk Road on horse and camel, and years spent living, working and travelling across Central Asia and Iran. Her Kazakh riding boots, of soft leather in a traditional pattern, catch my eye as she speaks.

In the New Year I'm on the Pashtu course. I devour the daily lessons and learn new words in the evening. Our charming Afghan teacher devises the curriculum on a week-by-week basis (the most recent textbook was produced in 1880, at the time of the second Anglo-Afghan war). I'm chuffed to be learning Pashtu, and excited about the coming deployment. I can't believe I haven't done this earlier during my time in the Army. As the deployment draws closer I make plans to attend a longer, eighteen-month Pashtu course on my return from Operation Herrick, the Afghanistan deployment, and afterwards to spend maybe a couple of years with the Army as an interpreter in Afghanistan.

*

'Prepare for action!' hollers the jumpmaster.

I'm in a Hercules above Salisbury Plain, deafened by the drone of the engines and pulled into the canvas troop seats by the weight of the parachute on my back. Though qualified as a military parachutist, I haven't jumped for a couple of years. Before deploying I need to do a couple of refresher jumps in order to get an extra few pounds of daily 'Para pay'.

Standing up with a slight wobble, I fasten the chin strap of my para helmet and attach my rucksack to the pair of quick-release hooks on my chest harness. The jumpmaster, a small lean man in a tight grey jumpsuit, clips a line from the back of my parachute onto the static line that will initiate my 'chute approximately four seconds after I jump. I'm number one on the port side. We number off with a shoulder slap passed down the line of eight men, ending with me.

'One OK, port stick OK,' I shout to the jumpmaster, with a thumb up.

I'm beckoned forward to the jump door. My stomach lurches. I take position: left foot forward, left arm holding the side of the door, right arm across the reserve 'chute on my chest. The wet greenness of Salisbury Plain whizzes past below me, incredibly close. Forcing the hint of a smile onto my face, I strive to appear utterly unafraid, knowing that the jumpmaster is watching for a flicker. Waves of adrenalin sweep up from my stomach. All my instincts are screaming at me to back away from the door. The red cautionary light comes on: jumping is imminent. The green above it flashes.

'GO!' screams the jumpmaster.

Launching myself out of the jump-door, I'm falling and

twisting, battered and wrenched from the aircraft by a screaming barrage of wind. Suddenly my chin is smashed onto my chest as my whole body is wracked upwards by the drag of my parachute and downwards by gravity. My 'chute is open. 'Thank fuck!' I garble in the floating stillness. Above me, my canopy is huge and green: 'Big, round and sound!' I shout in delighted repetition of the training mantra. Checking my air space, I look left, right and below. I steer away from the parachutist above me, gathering the canvas rigging lines and heaving them down into my chest. A slight twitch in the canopy pulls it forward and left. Looking down, I pull my rucksack quick-release strap; it falls for a couple of seconds, then jolts as the connecting rope takes the strain. I'm drifting forward and right; I take the rear risers and pull them down, squeezing them into my midriff. I'm still going forward, squeezing my legs and ankles tight together, and now I'm shooting sideways and the ground rushes up.

'Umph!' I'm bounced onto the ground, still moving; the wind's got my chute. Dragged bumping over the grass I fumble for the quick release: I break a rigging line and grind to a halt. My deflated canopy swirls around me.

'Thank fuck!' I gasp, genuinely grateful that I haven't broken my legs, and jubilant and exhilarated at having survived the mad risk of the last forty-five seconds. This mad risk, shared as a common experience, is the glue that holds the airborne forces together. Though I'm a Scots Guards officer, Para 'Toms' – private soldiers – that I've never met before will automatically make positive assumptions about me (and vice versa) on seeing the set of blue Para 'wings' on my shoulder.

Gathering up my 'chute, I run for the vehicle at the side of the drop zone. I need to get back to load up for the second jump of the day.

In the late afternoon, elated by two successful jumps, I drive away from RAF Lyneham. Stopping off at Lucy's for tea, my green combats (striped with Salisbury Plain's mud) and maroon beret take a verbal battering from her all-female household. But the doughnuts and lardy cake I've brought win some sympathy, and before departing Lucy and I make plans to go the cinema on the following evening.

Later that night, my euphoria at the jumping is cut short by a phone call from an Army friend.

'Leo, it's Chris . . . I've got some bad news – Rich Holmes has been killed. He was blown up in Al Amarah.'

Richard was our friend at Sandhurst. Deeply gentle and humane, he was the lynchpin of our platoon. His kindness, modesty and ability allowed him to never once be riled during our year of frequently exhausting and tedious training. He showed particular patience with the often-confused foreign Officer Cadets.

A week later the church, bathed in clear winter sunshine, is packed out. Mourners spill onto the grass outside, following the service on a video screen. I stand at the edge of the throng with other former platoon-mates. His closest friend from the platoon is in the church and with admirable composure does a short reading.

It's an accidental reunion of good friends, long unseen. We've not been together like this since the passing-out parade. We've all changed – a testament to the last four years. Some, dressed in suits, have recently left the Army; some are in Regimental Service dress with two or three medals; a couple, conspicuous with longer hair and lamb-chop side-burns, are now in the SAS. All of us have been in Iraq. Some will go again soon, for their second or third tour.

The professional devotion of our group allows us to focus on the comforting fact that Richard was killed doing a job he loved, among men he led with mutual respect and admiration. Such a good man, so selfless, so brave: surely his death is a reflection, a confirmation, of these qualities? We're soldiers, dedicated to soldiering and bound together by a simple ideal: the acceptance, pursuit even, of risk. We're loyal to our profession of choice and loyal beyond our own knowledge to our fellow soldiers. Moralising about the rights and wrongs of the Iraq war would at this moment be unthinkable, irrelevant. The fact that our friend was a victim of what we all know to be a disastrous and dishonest campaign lies dormant, unspoken. There is no outrage at his death, just a sad acceptance.

Outside on the grass, at the periphery of the mourners, I cannot begin to conceive what measure of grief his widow and family must be suffering at this moment inside the church, sitting next to the flag-draped coffin. I stick to small talk, in vain trying to avoid the horrible truth that our friend is being buried in the very place where he was married six months previously.

'So what's happening in Afghanistan?' Chris asks as we disperse from the church.

'Well, it's reconstruction really, you know, nation-building . . .' I answer, vacantly.

'So not like Iraq then?'

'No, thank god, nothing like Iraq.'

*

53

On the wet square of Goojerat Barracks in Colchester figures slowly gather in the chilly darkness, exchanging excited banter, hands thrust deep in the pockets of pale desert smocks. We're waiting for the bus to take us to Brize Norton in Oxfordshire, to catch a flight to Kabul and onwards. I feel good, really good. The lean simplicity of my previous travels in Afghanistan has returned: it's just me, my rucksack and my weapon, in the desert combats I'll wear constantly for the next few months.

CHAPTER 4

The Comprehensive Approach

April 2006: Southern Afghanistan

I sit just behind the Helmand Task Force Commander on the flight out to Kabul. I'm to be his Aide-de-Camp. I'm like an assistant, but I'm pleased as involvement at this senior level and the responsibility it brings should prove interesting. The Commander is a very likeable senior officer, unusually down to earth for his senior rank. He's in a tricky position: in addition to commanding an incredibly complex operation at its inception he's a newcomer to 16 Air Assault Brigade, of which the Task Force is mainly composed. The loyalty of most of the senior officers in the headquarters is bound to lie still with the Brigadier who's overseeing the whole thing at a higher level in Kabul.

The Commander hands me his copy of the Operational Order – the set of orders for the entire Task Force. 'Fuck me,' I think. 'This is it – these pages will determine the future of Helmand!' Our deployment is all over the press now and I can't help feeling excited to be at the epicentre of something so huge, important, maybe even historic, at its very beginning.

Signed off by the Commander, it's essentially the product of the precociously bright Chief of Staff, effectively his second-in-command. I take notes in order to remember the complex sequence of phases that it stipulates.

At the tactical level – for the troops on the ground – the plan is to use something called 'the Mosaic'. It demands that all British units be aware of all facets of Afghan society – the tribes, the economy and local politics – while working within it. There's a neat illustration resembling a Tudor rose.

Strategically, the plan for Helmand Province as a whole is based on 'the Comprehensive Approach'. This means the problems in Helmand – like opium production and lawlessness – will be dealt with in a comprehensive manner, from all angles.

I'm familiar with this jargon because in Colchester the headquarters personnel participated in 'joint' planning days, a chance for the military to get to know the representatives of the Foreign and Commonwealth Office (FCO) and the Department for International Development (DfID) who'll be working with us on the ground in Afghanistan. In outline, our intent is to improve security in Lashkar Gah, the provincial capital, allowing DfID to start practical development projects, while the FCO will focus on counter-narcotics and improving governance. An 'inkspot' – a security haven – will therefore be established in which life can return to normal. If all goes to plan security, development and governance will go hand-in-hand in the push to reconstruct civil society. Success lies ultimately in depriving opium barons and insurgents of their basis of support by winning the hearts and minds of the civil population. As success is consolidated, the inkspot will grow.

While a frequent practical term of reference for this sort of

campaign is the successful British counter-insurgency conducted in Malaya in the 1950s, the doctrine behind the Comprehensive Approach is contained in a little glossy manual
produced by the Ministry of Defence: *Operations other than
War.* In Colchester the bookish Colonel in charge of its production dished out copies and gave us a slide-show of vivid
diagrams illustrating its content. My favourite was a colourful multi-stranded rope representing the simultaneity and
interdependence of each 'Line of Operation'.

Some of our partners in the Comprehensive Approach
struck me as unlikely Afghan operators but seemed to have
hidden depths. The DfID woman in charge of development
in Helmand, with her fake plastic fingernails glued on
wonkily, had spent the previous eight years sinking wells in
Nigeria.

'Improving livelihoods is the key,' she told me over a vol-
au-vent during our lunch break. The statistics were shock-
ing. Afghanistan is one of the least developed countries in
the world, where a majority of the population lacks access to
electricity and clean drinking water, 20 per cent of children
die before the age of five, and more than 70 per cent of the
population are illiterate. Despite this she was optimistic.

'We've got ninety million pounds this year to spend on
the National Development Strategy so we should make
progress . . .'

As she detailed how livelihoods might be improved
through 'microfinance lending' and 'Quick Impact Projects',
I shared her enthusiasm.

The counter-narcotics part of the plan was also upbeat
despite the colossal challenge: Afghanistan's economy

depends on poppy-growing, producing 90 per cent of the world's opium.

'We won't be too hasty, we'll promote alternatives,' said the representative from the Foreign Office. He couldn't name the alternative crop to poppy but the plan seemed pretty sensible: 'an eight-strand strategy,' he said, starting with 'public information' leading to 'alternative livelihoods' and 'eventual eradication'. I found this fascinating and left the planning day sharing the earnest optimism of our 'Joint' partners.

Handing back the orders to the Commander, I accept a smoked-salmon sandwich, which he kindly offers from his lunchbox. The fact that he's prepared to divvy-up his packed lunch is a good sign.

Landing in Kabul, we're greeted by the sparkling white tops of the surrounding mountains. It's April, so the morning is cool and the air is clear, almost crisp. An abundance of multinational fighter jets and helicopters are lined up on the tarmac. In the cookhouse there are thirty different signing-in books: one for each nationality in the Coalition. I wonder what it is the Bulgarians do, and am entertained to see a solitary Icelandic soldier guarding the front gate alongside some Italians. The French seem especially ornamental and pose absurdly in their too-short combat trousers. These over-clean staff officers are the physical opposite of the Afghans whose city they live in. As a body they are bloated and ineffectual. Their only value lies in the veneer of international inclusivity which they lend the Coalition. They represent the worst aspect of the international force. Thankfully I'll be getting well away from them; there's no room for their sort in Helmand.

In a Hercules transport plane to Kandahar, we're crammed into the hammock-like canvas seats by the RAF crew. The recollection of doing parachute jumps inspires a brief surge of exhilaration as we file in through the tailgate. I imagine myself as a paratrooper in some heroic Second World War operation and wonder if the rumours of there being a 'lob-on' – a para jump – in Helmand will materialise. The RAF loadmasters hand out squashy yellow earplugs and try to look cool in their flying suits. As we make a grinding ascent over Kabul the G-force drives our bodies downwards. Dazed by the deafening noise and vibration of the turbo propellers, some of us sleep, some read, others try to look nonchalant. I crane my neck to see out of the circular window. Distinct among the mass of ramshackle buildings closeted by sudden, sheer hills is the bombed-out shell of King Zahir Shah's old palace, Dar-ul-Aman. Surely this is a symbol, related to the reconstructive nature of our mission? I spend a few moments trying to concoct an appropriate metaphor before my mind wanders.

Seeing Kabul from the air brings to my mind's eye the aerial photograph that two weeks previously my Pashtu teacher in Beaconsfield had laid out before me. Homesick, he had acquired the photo from a friend in the MoD so that he might locate his home. On the floor of his office the map drew us in as he showed me his home, his school and where he used to eat ice cream and go to the cinema. I was intrigued to locate, with his help, Hotel Spinzar – a crumbling pre-Soviet pseudo-European tower where I'd stayed the previous autumn. I wonder if what I'd seen on his map is still standing below me, or if it's become sadly fictitious under the horrific rocket barrages fired by the Mujahideen factions as they turned against one another after their capture of the city from the Soviet puppet government in 1993.

Descending into Kandahar, the beige monotony of the ground is dotted with crooked verdant rectangles of agricultural land gathered about glistening irrigation channels. Everything else is barren, flat and dusty. The distant jagged mountains are devoid of the softening snow-caps seen around Kabul.

In Kandahar Air Field (known as KAF) the phenomenal scale of the US war machine announces itself with an array of hardware that easily dwarfs that in Kabul. A single row of USAF Black Hawk, Chinook or Apache helicopters outnumbers the entire British complement.

Away from the asphalt of the runway, a mini-America has been spookily recreated. KFC, Subway, Pizza Hut and Tim Horton's peddle their junk food to the homesick. The Green Bean Café sells Frappucinos for four dollars a go. The PX (military supermarket) is crammed with everything one might want for a comfortable and productive war-on-terror: pistol holsters (I opt for a black leather leg holster as used by NYPD), chewing tobacco, and T-shirts publicising the wearer's participation in 'Operation Enduring Freedom' with the reverse side advocating the opening of a can of 'whoop ass'.

The inhabitants of this bizarre mini-city are its greatest fascination. Hundreds of civilians are employed by the vast administrative machine that is required to feed, clean, wash the laundry of and process the shit of every soldier. For this task the American mega-corporation Kellogg Brown and Root employs the purest rednecks and poorest blacks and

Hispanics. Many have been in KAF since its inception as a US base of operations five years ago, and are looking forward to owning their own homes or sending their children to college on the back of it.

Numerous cavernous DFACs (dining facilities) churn out lobster and T-bone steaks, cheeseburgers and cookies with ice cream. Fridges hold free soft drinks and M&Ms. This is an unimagined luxury for the British soldier, sustained on 'one choice only' – probably curry or shepherd's pie and polystyrene sponge cake. The British troops staying at Kandahar before deploying to Helmand will briefly enjoy this catering at a cost of 44 dollars per day per soldier to the MoD.

The welfare facilities provided for the US military also come as a revelation to the Brits arriving in Kandahar. The Morale, Welfare and Relaxation centre (MWR) offers a cinema, a dance hall, dozens of computer play-stations, pool tables and free coffee and popcorn. In the evenings groups of blacks play dominoes, while the Hispanics dance salsa. Everyone else munches popcorn or chewing tobacco, watching noisy Hollywood violence. Men and women are both dressed in combats or identical grey Army sports shirts and shorts, some with a yellow reflector band clipped about their waist to ensure a safe walk back to their tent at the evening's close. Over the road in the vast gymnasium great heavy-limbed, lumbering, jar-headed men pump iron. Outside, next to the gym, is an immaculate floodlit basketball court, spoilt only by the dust and sewerage stench whipped up by an incessant south-westerly wind.

The MWR provides its users with a taste of the US homeland. It's a monument to a collective attempt to forget that the nearest town is Kandahar and not Kansas. Everyone, however, even those in sports kit, carries a perpetual reminder of the reality. Their weapon, probably a 9mm pistol, long M16 rifle or stocky M4, slung under a shoulder or leaning intimately on a leg, is never more than an arm's reach away.

The following day we set out with the new headquarters staff to 'recce' Lashkar Gah, where the HQ will eventually be located. We're on a pair of Chinooks (they always work in twos). The door gunner trails his legs off the back of the rear ramp and waves to the pilot of the second 'bird'. I think of the Americans offending Muslim sensibilities in Mogadishu with their dangling footsoles, but the desert whizzing past fifty feet below seems bereft of inhabitants.

The camp at Lashkar Gah is a muddled building site of yellow half-cylindrical Temporarily Deployable Accommodation (TDA) tents clustered around a few flat-roofed concrete buildings. There's a small US Provincial Reconstruction Team (PRT) here who'll shortly hand over to British troops. Portakabin accommodation is also being constructed for the FCO and DfID staff that will be part of the Helmand Task Force. Unlike the Army, for some reason, they'll not live in the TDA. It's perhaps not up to their required standard of comfort. The camp is protected by the Texas National Guard.

Moving away from the gaggle of the headquarters, I'm drawn to the vivid colours of a patch of floral garden. The gardener, a wizened man with a white beard and faded prayer cap on the back of his head, stands upright from the flowerbeds as I approach. We have a stilted Pashtu conversation. Delighted to be able to share his passion, he names each type of flower, which I forget immediately on hearing. He asks me if I'm coming back, and I hope I will if only to enjoy the garden further. Asking him to repeat his name, I write it in my notebook: Sayyid Shah. Later I wonder why he had not grown kitchen vegetables as a source of a little extra income or nourishment. This Afghan devotion to flowers (*Gul*) is widespread and sincere. In Afghanistan the previous autumn I'd seen men wearing flowers behind their ears, and floral decorations ubiquitous in restaurants and vehicles.

Back in Kandahar I take advantage of the fact that the Commander is away in Kabul for the day to zero my rifle. In the Commander's four-wheel drive I turn up at the range to find three US Special Forces and an FBI agent. The Special Forces have neatly groomed beards, climbing boots and mixed clothes, some civilian beige, some old issue US camouflage – the stuff with wavy brown and beige lines rather than the new greyish computer-generated 'visual white noise' kit. I like the old stuff better. The FBI guy gives me some ammo, as I'm concerned about having to account for my own (this range is closed by the Brits to their own troops for not meeting petty MoD health and safety regulations, so none of the HQ have zeroed their weapons yet). The mag from his M4 fits my SA80 A2 – 'Yay for NATO,' he chuckles. The senior SF guy, who quickly introduces himself, lends me his binoculars. I expend three mags correcting my sight and then accept their offer to fire the M4. I like it more than my weapon; it's lighter, has a better scope and less recoil. They fire mine and take photos. The FBI guy shows me his lead-tipped 5.56 rounds. With a soft nose they have the dum-dum effect of a small entry, large exit wound. Luckily, he says, though forbidden for use by conventional troops, they're legal for him. The senior SF bloke gives me his business card before leaving and asks if they can come along if there's an operational parachute jump. 'Just gimme me a call, Leo. I'd love to hop and pop with you guys.'

While I'm cleaning my rifle five minutes later their four-wheel drive returns and one of the SF guys jumps out. Embarrassed at his carelessness, he picks up a rifle magazine he's left on the firing point.

On his return from Kabul the Commander is summoned by the Governor of Helmand. The Pathfinder Platoon, a recon-naissance unit, have had a contact (live rounds being fired) involving the police near Now Zad, a small town in the north of the Province. This is a 'blue-on-blue' – friendly forces shooting at each other by mistake – and the Governor wants an explanation. We jump onto a Chinook, overfly the site of the contact and then land at FOB (Forward Operating Base) Price, the Pathfinder base near Gereshk.

In a blacked-out operations room housed in a low con-crete building the Commander is briefed by the platoon sergeant, a weather-beaten man in a faded green T-shirt. Over a map board, he explains that the contact was superfi-cially the result of the police mistaking the British for a Tal-iban convoy: 'The patrol went into an overnight lie-up position here,' he says, pointing with a pencil to a blue pin in the map, near Now Zad.

'In the morning they were approaching the town and were fired on by the police. They returned fire, and one of the wagons rolled when it swerved during the initial contact so they fired the Milan [anti-tank missile] into it to prevent the ECM [Electronic Counter Measure: used to prevent hostile detonation of improvised bombs by remote radio control] equipment getting nicked.' He pauses, rubbing his bald repeatedly sunburnt head, then continues: 'There was a bit of a stand-off, then everyone realised what was happening and things calmed down. We had no casualties but two policemen were injured so our guys helped patch them up.'

'So, mistaken identity was the cause, was it?' asks the Commander pensively.

'Well, boss, ICOM hits [intercepted radio communications] indicated that the police thought the patrol was after their opium stash. I reckon they opened fire as a delaying tactic.'

'Jesus,' I think, 'this is a serious can of worms.' The depth of narco-corruption in Helmand Province must be catastrophic if even those charged with upholding the law are complicit in the opium industry. It's a daunting revelation of the enormity of the task facing us, especially as we're supposed to be working jointly with the Afghan police. How on earth can we make them un-corrupt? Probably the answer lies in retraining and improved salaries, but given that Helmand's entire economy is opium-reliant, an alternative to poppy is badly needed. Whatever the solution, it's going to involve a massive, fundamental change in Helmand's economy and government and, crucially, the loyalty of its people. It's something that'll take years, not months, to put right. However, I'm intrigued rather than exasperated by the problem; after all, we've got the Comprehensive Approach.

This is the first contact for British troops in Helmand Province and the platoon sergeant seems chuffed by all the attention. Outside, we bid farewell and scurry towards the waiting Chinook. He gives us a wave, shading his eyes from the afternoon sun, then draws on a cigarette.

Onboard the Chinook I guzzle a few half-litre bottles of mineral water, trying to stay hydrated. The water is warm and the air, already hot, is heated more by the Chinook engines. I feel slightly sick.

Landing in Lashkar Gah, we're met by a British Major, a soft-ly spoken northerner who commands the troops due to take over the Provincial Reconstruction Team role from the Americans. He tells us that they're patrolling the town to a limited extent and yesterday suffered a suicide-vehicle bombing at the front gate in which two soldiers were injured. One has a minor arm wound; the other had part of his ear blown off.

After bundling into a convoy of three Snatch wagons, we head out of camp towards the Governor's compound. Keen to see the town, I get up on 'top-cover' (this involves standing out of a trapdoor in the roof of the vehicle). Next to me, revealed by the hair bun under her helmet, is a young woman. I'm surprised at this, given that Afghan women are invisible to us except for the odd glimpse of a burqa scurry-ing away, or stepping quickly back behind a door, after scooping up a child or two. I wonder how the locals of Lashkar Gah feel about it. Driving through the town, though, no one seems perturbed and my top-cover buddy gets stuck in to giving lots of 'steer away' hand signals to passing cars.

The men and children of Lashkar Gah are a deeply striking bunch, fulfilling every stereotype of hawk-nosed, swarthy, handsome Pashtuns. Brightly clothed, barefooted children wave happily, their kohl-lined eyes flashing under thick black hair. The streets are broad and well maintained and the town has a solid feel to it. Much of this is the legacy of capital injected in the 1960s from an American-sponsored cotton cultivation programme.

At the Governor's headquarters, a large rambling pile right on the edge of the Helmand River, the Commander and I dismount. Just in our combats, without weapons, we're ushered into a waiting room by a lean, ugly British bloke with beige fatigues and a stubby little machine gun. He's an employee of the private military company protecting the Governor. The waiting room has a high ceiling and is adorned with painted panels depicting renowned highlights of Afghanistan: the Shrine at Mazar-e-Sharif, the Salang Tunnel, the minaret of Djam and others. They have a naive charm about them, probably unintended by the artist.

Tom Tugendhat arrives: a Brit in his early thirties, he's the Governor's special adviser. He's surprisingly dapper in a blue gingham shirt. With unconvincing gravitas he says that the Governor has now calmed down, having earlier been furious about the Pathfinder contact. Still, this is definitely a bollocking; our host has not yet arrived, we are standing and have not been offered any refreshment. According to the Afghan concept of hospitality, such treatment, in normal circumstances, would be unthinkable and shameful.

Finally the Governor, Engineer Daoud, arrives. We all shake hands and sit down. Like his townsmen outside, the

Governor is a striking individual with a long, elegant nose, neatly clipped beard and a calm countenance.

'Let me start with a proverb,' he says slowly. His English is well pronounced and deliberate. He pauses often, considering his next sentence. 'Only those who are working make mistakes. I was angry when I heard of this incident but I know those involved were acting in good faith.'

The Commander relates his version of events, omitting the bit about the police deliberately firing on the British patrol and the fact that it's a vivid illustration of police corruption.

The Governor nods his head. 'I would like to request an investigation into the causes of the incident.'

He's no fool and is bound to be aware that events were a bit more complicated than described.

'. . . Also I need more police.'

Given that the police force is involved in the opium business, it's hardly surprising their impact is limited and he feels he needs more. The Commander agrees that this would be sensible. The Governor then makes his final and most ambitious request of the Commander.

'The Taliban have occupied a village and closed its school in Baghran. We must try to re-establish law and order and re-open the school . . .' The Governor continues calmly: 'Could you send your troops?'

At the furthest northern part of Helmand, the rugged Baghran valley lies high in the foothills of the Kindu Kush.

The Commander says he'll look into it and assures the Governor that we're here to support him. By the end of the meeting the atmosphere, having become increasingly amicable, is hearty and friendly.

Back in camp I phone through the message about Baghran, but the Operations Officer – in charge of controlling current operations – is vexed. He's busy producing computer slides for the daily evening update in the headquarters, and says reluctantly that he'll look into it.

Later in the afternoon, the Commander is determined to come up with a solution to the policing problem in Helmand. It's clear they're untrustworthy and ineffectual. We need to sort it out because the military will need to work alongside them. On a whiteboard, the Commander brainstorms the problem with the help of Tom Tugendhat, the Major commanding the Provincial Reconstruction Team and the FCO police adviser. I take notes. It's an overwhelming prospect: a new police force will require selection and training and a huge amount of resources to clothe, equip, feed and accommodate them.

'Let's have an *auxiliary* police force!' declares the Commander, scribbling feverishly onto the whiteboard. 'Something for the interim, until a proper force is ready to take over.'

'There should be enough money in the FCO budget,' says Tugendhat, nodding, 'for, let's say, twenty-four men per district? They can be casual auxiliaries at first and get special training later on . . . Like the seed of a new force.'

'But they *must* be selected by the community,' continues the Commander, 'so they have the trust of the people. In fact they'd be *Community Police*,' he concludes with a flourish of his pen.

A list of required kit is hastily drawn up on the whiteboard. The plan is concluded.

'I'll present it to the Governor,' says Tugendhat, 'but I'm sure he'll be happy.'

'This is the way to do it,' I think. 'Action this Day!'

The FCO police adviser has been quiet. Perhaps it's an apt reflection of the FCO's practically non-existent police strategy up until now. The Germans are supposed to be sorting out policing at a national level, and at the provincial level in Helmand it's the FCO's bag, but nothing seems to have been achieved. Having said that, maybe this new plan is folly and we're blundering after a solution emboldened by our ignorance. There've been no Afghans at the meeting and it's probably too complex a problem to solve in half an hour in front of a whiteboard. But at least the Commander's doing something practical, which is more than the FCO have even tried.

That evening at supper in the DFAC I sit with Tom Tugendhat, who's living in the camp until he gets a safe house in town. He takes monumental pleasure in devouring a pair of Snickers ice-cream bars- a luxury available only in American DFACs, which won't be there when the Brits formally take over the camp and run the catering in a couple of weeks' time.

Tugendhat's role in Lashkar Gah harks back to the days of political officers or 'Residents' in British Colonial India – experts who, having spent probably their entire lives in the region, resided with the local ruler in order to advise, coerce and persuade in accordance with the central government's intent. The ability of a single confident Brit to discreetly control the reins of local governance was the necessary foundation of the entire imperial project. In his unique position, Tugendhat is paid by the FCO and wields considerable influence with the Governor, whom he previously knew by association in Kabul where the Governor (an engineer by profession) was working for the United Nations. On accepting the governorship of Helmand from President Karzai, Engineer Daoud (professional titles are assiduously used in Afghanistan as a status marker) requested that the bright young orientalist come with him. The current situation is of course very different to the imperial project, but Tugendhat's influence is immeasurably more efficient, discreet and beneficial than that of any number of conventional troops trying to have a political effect.

'If I'm to maintain such a high standard of cuisine in my new house,' he says, scrunching up his ice-cream wrapper with a grin, 'I'll have to employ a Hazara chef!'

From the high Hindu Kush, such people with their reputation for good cooking are a rarity in the remote Pashtun south.

That night, the Commander gamely accepts an invitation from the 'other agencies' to an illicit glass of wine that's been brought from the UK, secreted deep in the luggage of an overconfident FCO girl. We sit in a group between their new Portakabins on a circle of plastic garden chairs. A pallid, sincere Finnish girl from DfID describes her experiences of having amoebic dysentery in Sarajevo. The FCO police adviser tells me he's sad to be leaving soon. The likelihood of the Governor receiving an armoured car from the FCO is also discussed. With no thirst for the wine I go to find a brew.

In the DFAC the troops are having a quiz night. Being Artillery, rather than Infantry, there are girls present and they're all in civilian clothing: shiny tracksuit trousers or jeans, football tops or trendy T-shirts. They're healthily sun-burnt and defiantly good-humoured. I can sense a collective feeling of relief and elation that no one was killed in yester-day's attack. A close shave having passed, morale is surging. As they huddle around the plastic tables, conferring in their teams and drinking cans of soda, I immediately feel a deep liking for them all. I make a cup of tea and leave them to it.

The following morning we're due to return to KAF. The Governor's coming with us – he's got an appointment to have his back seen to at the excellent Dutch hospital there. Waiting for the helicopter, I climb up into one of the corner guard-towers on the perimeter.

The inside smells of urine and has Spanish graffiti scrawled across the grey walls. A Texas National Guardsman sits on a plastic garden chair in the middle of the concrete floor, facing a heavy machine gun pointing ominously out of the narrow window, wrapped in a belt of bullets. His rifle leans in the corner.

'I've been in this tower for the last four hours,' Ramez tells me. With eight more hours to go, I assume he's bored out of his mind, but he loves it.

Eager to talk, he joins me at the window. 'I'm glad to be serving in Afghanistan; I lost weight and learnt a lot. I want to help these people,' he says, pointing a chubby finger through the small window. 'I'll tell my children about it when they're older. I'll tell them that they shot at us and we had to shoot back. I dunno . . . It's maybe hard for them to understand.'

Wishing him a safe tour, I shake his hand and climb down the stepladder.

On the Chinook the Governor and his two Afghan secretaries are thrilled by the experience and take numerous photos. In camp I organise lunch in the vast main American DFAC. After chatting up the Filipino table-clearer I manage to get a bunch of grapes put in the middle of the table, but this improvement cannot mask the incongruity of the situation: the Governor gingerly chewing a cheeseburger next to the Commander and the Chief of Staff. In an odd reversal of roles, the Governor looks much less awesome than yesterday. Despite being of local origin, he's spent a lot of time in Kabul so in Helmand his power base – his ability to exploit personal connections to achieve things – is limited. In a country where family, kin and tribe are of paramount importance in political affairs, it's suddenly very clear that he's relying on us to support his position. He's a bit like the Iraqi Sheikh I met eighteen months ago but on a grander scale. It's hardly surprising, then, that he wants us to bolster his authority in the chaotic north of Helmand. Giving up with the cheeseburger, the Governor pops a grape into his mouth, his countenance remaining serene.

With the north emerging as an area of interest, the Commander and I go on a recce to FOB Robinson (named after a US fatality). It's a ramshackle collection of mud buildings, metal storage containers and vehicles, encircled by a vast wall of earth-filled barrier blocks. We drop off at around midnight from a US Chinook crammed with re-supplies, and with a crouching half-run find our way out of the biting wall of dust kicked up by the Chinook's twin rotors.

We get a brief from a Canadian company commander. He

says they've recently done an operation which failed to find a local opium baron. The good news, however, is that he's since been killed by an American Hellfire missile. In the last month they've done some patrolling near the town in their Light Armoured Vehicles (LAVs), and have had two KIA (killed in action): one was a result of blue-on-blue, the other was an officer who got a hatchet in the head, having taken his helmet off while in a local village. The attacker was shot dead. Significantly, in March there was a full-on frontal assault on the FOB from two directions simultaneously, initiated by RPGs (rocket-propelled grenades) fired in a volley. This is clearly serious stuff and says a great deal about the level of skill and commitment of the Taliban – if that's who the enemy is. He explains that the US Special Forces team working from the FOB have been twitchy as hell since losing two guys a couple of weeks ago in an ambush. During their retreat, under enemy fire, they called in air strikes which dropped a total of thirteen 500 lb J-DAM bombs – an incredible amount of destructive ordnance. Consequently they now stay mainly in the FOB, sometimes going out for unambitious local operations such as searching the nearest villages.

A few hours later, following a freezing night of broken sleep in my jungle sleeping bag next to a Canadian armoured vehicle, I head over to the Afghan National Army (ANA) compound with the Commander. As we walk towards the watchtowers overlooking the Helmand River a gaggle of grubby, smiling ANA greet us. They wear soiled green camouflage fatigues donated by the US and plastic sandals or inferior black leather boots. I ask them in Urdu how they are.

'We're fine,' replies the most confident, advancing slightly from the group. 'But we want to be relieved and return to Herat, our base.'

In the very north-west of Afghanistan, this ancient city with a great poetic and artistic tradition has long been renowned for its pleasant climate.

'We don't mind living here,' he says, pointing at the ramshackle watchtowers where they eat and sleep, 'and the river is pleasant for bathing, but we miss our home.'

Declining tea, we move over to a small mud-walled compound, home to the American Training Team. They're from the Alabama National Guard and their role is to mentor the ANA and facilitate joint operations with the other troops in the FOB. Two of them are on the flat roof glumly watching the fat orange sun come up. They say they've been pretty much stuck in the FOB since the Special Forces suffered the two fatalities. They seem pretty disappointed to be here, but one of them immediately perks up when I ask him about the .38 sporting rifle slung under his arm, giving him the air of a professional hunter. He flicks off the scope cap and puts it up to my shoulder. I gain a sight picture and scan the glistening green edges of the Helmand River. I imagine him sniping an Afghan in the head with it but can't bring myself to ask the question.

Back at the Canadian armoured vehicles, an athletic black guy brings over some pop-tarts for breakfast. He's the commander of the US Special Forces team. He's clearly rattled by recent events and is keen to leave. He hates the Afghans.

'I just wanna get away from these people. You never know what they're thinking . . .'

As we wait for the helicopter just outside the FOB, the Commander muses on how to deal with Sangin. He's thinking out loud: 'We'll not get sucked in to Sangin, I'll tell the Paras to contain it and not get sucked in . . .'

Beside us, adjacent to the FOB's defensive tangle of razor wire and earthen wall, is a field of poppy plants, their white and purple flowers quivering in the slight wind. In the field two bodies are bent double, busily weeding. The crop smells sweet and in a few days will be harvested of its opiate gum.

CHAPTER 5

With the Afghans

April 2006: Helmand Province, Afghanistan

Three weeks later I'm already bored with being based in the
headquarters. Doing recces with the Commander is fun but
I spend a lot of time hanging onto his coat-tails in the vast
air-conditioned headquarters tent, under ghastly yellow tube
lighting and among ranks of computers manned by diligent
but very dull staff officers. I physically detest it and know
that I'll never be able to cut around on the ground in this job.
It represents the absolute opposite of what I want to experience in Afghanistan. Luckily, there's an empty slot in the
team that'll be embedded with the ANA (Afghan National
Army) and if I play the language card I reckon I've a good
chance of being allowed to go. The Commander doesn't
really need an ADC anyway. There's no shortage of brown-
nosing staff officers willing to make his cups of tea.

As we leave the Dutch hospital in Kandahar after visiting
two Pathfinder casualties injured by a land mine, the Commander seems in reflective mood. I reckon it's a good time to
ask to be moved, and I'm quietly delighted when he agrees to
my request without hesitation.

Feeling optimistic, I lug my kit from the headquarters

tents (eight men in each tent with air-con) to a vast hundred-man transit tent. Like gigantic budget marquees, these tents are designed to accommodate all new arrivals during their brief stay in KAF before they deploy 'forward'. I dump my kit on an empty bunk. There are some Dutch troops on one side and female nurses on the other. Most of these nurses won't deploy forward at all. As some joker points out, Kandahar for them should more suitably be renamed 'Kandaraki' in homage to the type of Club 18–30 destinations of which they're fond.

Among a gaggle of T-shirted troops sitting on a crooked square of metal bunk-beds I meet Company Sergeant-Major Johnstone. He's an Edinburgh man in his early thirties with greying temples. With cropped hair and a broad grin, there's a whiff of the violent jock about him. A confident sparkle in his eyes seems to say, 'I'm happy with discomfort, squalor and violence, I've lived through them all and have no fear of them.' Although he's from the Army Air Corps he's an Infantry specialist and has just completed a six-month tour instructing Iraqi Officer Cadets at the Al Rustamiyah Officer Training Academy, known as the 'Baghdad Sandhurst'. During frequent patrols into the city – the epicentre of Iraq's insurgent, sectarian and all other types of violence – he saw a great deal of action, firing six hundred rounds in six months. The CSM and I will mentor a company (approximately sixty men) of ANA soldiers. Our purpose will be to further train and conduct operations with these freshly trained troops newly arrived from Kabul Military Training Centre, where they complete a basic six-month infantry course.

Johnstone tells me that the Mentoring Team has been in

theatre a couple of weeks and is composed of volunteers who responded to a trawl across the Army, including the Territorial Army. It's the MoD's clever way of dealing with an overstretched Army: an additional unit is effectively created by borrowing men from those already established. The benefit, however, is that the Mentoring Team's range of experience is diverse: some, like Johnstone himself, have returned recently from Iraq, while others left the regular Army a dozen years ago. There's about thirty men in all. Because the team is not a normal unit there's been a cock-up with equipment. The usual operational stuff that any unit would take for granted has not been allocated and there's simply no extra materiel in theatre. Consequently the team currently has no radios, no night-vision equipment, no heavy machine guns and no medical supplies. I assure him someone in HQ is bound to be dealing with this problem.

The Afghan battalion which we'll mentor has not yet arrived from Kabul, so we make use of the time to conduct our own training. The medic, Sergeant Stoddart, a TA Geordie whose last operational tour was 'Gulf War One', gives us first-aid lessons in the shade of the concrete bomb shelters outside our tents. After the lesson I blag a load of plasti-cuffs for use as tourniquets from a sympathetic engineer who has a few extra packets.

An unwelcome return to the bomb shelters is made in the horribly early hours of the following morning. A double bang reverberates through the tent, shaking me awake.

'Oh God,' I groan, disgusted at the prospect of having to get out of bed.

The siren cranks up. It's either a mortar or a rocket attack.

Sliding out of bed, I put my helmet on and make for the hard cover, pulling on my body armour. Inside the shelter the Dutch are smoking excitedly, looking ridiculous in the pyjamas/body-armour/helmet combination. I happily deprive myself of the full benefit of the shelter to avoid their cigarette smoke. Returning to the tent after the all-clear has sounded, I'm piqued to see that others have slept through the whole thing.

In the morning the nurses sunbathe and flaunt their ill-advised tattoos, while the advance party of 3 Para ride around on their quad bikes. The nurses have gained sudden desirability purely due to their location. There's a least one hundred blokes to every one girl in KAF.

The Kandak ('battalion' in Dari) having arrived from Kabul, we go to meet them in Camp Shirzai, about a kilometre away from KAF. The troops are mustered into a hollow square, more than four hundred of them, waiting for General Raufi, the Commander of 205 Corps, which has been assigned to Helmand Province. We stand to the flanks. The Afghan officers at this distance are indistinguishable from the men, all massed together in their dark green camouflage fatigues and green berets. As the General approaches, a grey-beard Sergeant Major brings them to attention; they slide their left heels together with their right, Soviet style.

The General, saluting, goose-steps into the middle of the hollow square and begins a speech. He says every sentence twice, once in Pashtu and once in Dari, my interpreter relaying the meaning. The troops are congratulated on the completion of their training and told to expect a hard campaign against the enemies of Afghanistan. Those who have gone absent – apparently more than a hundred in the last four days – are savagely belittled. This harangue has been going for ten minutes when my interpreter goes silent. I don't bother to prompt a restart. After a further ten minutes attention among the troops has diminished and those in the rear ranks, who can't be seen by the General, rest on their haunches. I'm eager to get among these ranks of scruffy troops and make an impact. We've clearly got our work cut out, with deserters leaving in droves, and our team like a rag-tag Afghan version of *The Wild Geese*. Despite this, however, I'm optimistic; a good bit of British Army banter should be able to turn their morale around.

Unable to find the HQ company commander (whom I'll mentor), I depart for KAF with Will, another Captain, driving the Ford Ranger which we've borrowed from the ANA. There seems to be an abundance of these US-supplied pick-up trucks in Shirzai – which is lucky, as ours are (hopefully) waiting for us in Helmand. Unconcerned about the short distance we have to travel, we chuck our kit onto the back seat – but then, as we're approaching the front gate of KAF, a huge whooshing wall of flame suddenly explodes directly to our front.

'Fucking hell! Get your kit on!' I shout, as Will slams on the brakes.

Jumping out, I scramble on my webbing vest, ram on my helmet, cock my weapon and look around in case a further attack is imminent. Apart from the shouting of the soldiers at the gate, there's nothing unusual apparent. I feel dangerously exposed.

'Let's get back in the wire!'

We leap back into the Ranger and scream towards the gate, now suddenly more concerned at the prospect of being shot as suicide bombers in our beige ANA wagon by the terrified Canadian gate guard.

A few days later we've moved to Helmand. We're in Camp Tombstone, a tiny Amercan-run compound that accommodates the engineers building Shoraback, a sprawling brigade-sized camp for five thousand men, next door. Tombstone is a cushy little camp: there's a pukka American DFAC, and cabins for accommodation rather than tents. The officers have their own dormitories, as do the sergeants and private soldiers. We're packed in like sardines but the air-con blower keeps it cool, and an array of home-made furniture, constructed from plywood salvaged from a half-constructed cabin next door, gives it a homely atmosphere. I'm on a top bunk above Will and next to Jim.

At 0500 I slide off my bunk and use my newly purchased shelving unit as a step down. I paid 20 dollars to one of the carpenters working next door for the lavish unit – designed to hold a TV and stereo system, it's currently housing our webbing vests, helmets and body armour. It reminds me that Will hasn't yet repaid me his half of the 20 dollars. Having silently put on my trainers and PT kit, I leave the sleeping dorm and run laps around the absurdly small inner perimeter of Tombstone. The sun is already on the rise and after about 0600 running is intolerable due to the heat and the dust carried on the wind from Camp Bastion, being built to house the main British contingent and still under construction five hundred metres away. Half an hour later, drenched

Iraq. Pleased with my combats, the Sheikh takes a fag break.

Iraq. With elders of Basra's Tribal Council, who gather to resolve disputes by applying traditional tribal law.

London. At the gilded epicentre of the establishment: the Officers' Mess at 'Jimmy's' – St James's Palace.

London. The Changing of the Guard: I'm very smart but very bored.

Pakistan. In the far north, near the Afghan border, my guide pegs down his horse for the night.

Pakistan. A brief taste of the frontier.

A Hazara man (left) and a Pashtun man crippled by one of the millions of land-mines scattered across Afghanistan (right) seek alms outside the mausoleum of Ali (the Prophet Mohammad's son-in-law) in Mazar-e-Sharif, northern Afghanistan.

A Wakhi shepherd boy, near the Wakhan Corridor, northern Pakistan. Parcels of clothing from international relief agencies often result in colourful incongruity.

Embedded in the Afghan National Army (ANA). The faces of Captain Hameed's men illustrate the pan-ethnic mix of Tajik, Pashtun, and Uzbek designed to make the ANA non-sectarian and representative of the Afghan nation.

In the 'Desert of Death'. Advancing to seize and occupy Sangin, with my 'Snatch' wagon – an armoured Land-Rover hopelessly ill-suited to desert conditions.

In the Sangin District Centre. Afghan men have a deep love of flowers, and use them frequently for decoration.

The calm before the storm: breakfast (milk whey and naan bread) with the ANA in the Sangin District Centre.

An impromptu tea party during a lull in operations. The ANA vehicle behind us (a repainted Ford Ranger pick-up truck) and the uniforms are donations from the USA.

On patrol in Sangin: determined to win hearts and minds, we've removed our sunglasses and helmets.

in sweat, I take a proper plumbed-in American shower, throw on my combats and, buckling my pistol onto my leg, head for the DFAC. Forgoing the pancakes, crispy bacon and grits option, I tuck into a bunch of fat red grapes and half a dozen green melon slices. My breakfast has, remarkably, been flown in from Dubai. It is a logistical wonder of the developed world that American soldiers in the Afghan desert can eat the same breakfast as those in the middle of the United States.

My next meal is of reassuringly local origin. Our Afghan company is now installed in Camp Shoraback next door, where I meet its commander. Captain Hameed is stocky, smooth-skinned and very clean. He has short, thick black hair and a neat, close beard. His combats, which are pressed, are tucked into new American desert boots which, I note, are in better repair than my own. Sitting cross-legged in his office we await the reappearance of Ramadan, the elfin tea boy, sent scurrying away with the metal teapot and a volley of shouted instructions. The Captain's office is a small room at the end of a long semi-cylindrical metal cabin which also serves as accommodation. It's essentially the same as ours, but without air conditioning. He seems fairly mystified by my presence, yet unwilling to summon the energy required to be fully inquisitive. He speaks Dari and via Tamim, my interpreter, assures me that he knows what he's doing.

'I've been fighting all my grown life with the Shura-i-Nazar [the Northern Alliance]. We fought the Taliban when no one else did.'

'I'm here purely to advise if necessary and will surely learn a great deal from you,' I reply, determined to be humble.

Thankfully, Ramadan reappears and serves glasses of boiling green tea and little Pakistani toffees. Captain Hameed is a Tajik from the Panjshir valley. Portraits of Ahmed Shah Masood furnish the office walls above me.

'Captain Hameed, I visited the mausoleum of the great Commander Masood while travelling in the Panjshir valley last year,' I reveal, hoping to impress.

He is unmoved, and does not respond. He seems to be taking it silently for granted, perhaps thinking, 'Hasn't everyone?'

His deputy, Abdul Qadir, and Company Sergeant-Major, Pir Ahmed, enter and shake my hand warmly. Both lithe, fine-featured Panjshiris, they settle beside us in anticipation of lunch. Ramadan places metal lunch trays before us, brought from the cookhouse. Each contains a little mutton stewed with potato, yoghurt, a mound of dark rice, and a thick, foot-long naan bread, crispy brown at the edges. Invoking the name of God with a whispered 'Bismillah!', my hosts and I break our bread and eat in silence. When my portion is finished, Captain Hameed places pieces of his own mutton on my tray until I am stuffed full. Reclining slightly, we have another round of tea, and conversation resumes. I broach the idea of doing some training which would be useful if the rumoured deployment to FOB Robinson occurs. Captain Hameed assures me that HQ Company isn't going anywhere as its duties are to guard the camp perimeter only. Less ambitiously, I suggest taking mugshots of his troops, for his records, to which he agrees. With Abdul Qadir and Pir Ahmed now fully reclined, I take my leave and, thanking him for lunch, leave them to sleep.

Tamim and I emerge blinking into the afternoon sun. It's

WITH THE AFGHANS

now almost 50 degrees and after our heavy lunch sleep is
inevitable. Leaving Tamim at the interpreter's hut, I trudge
back through the dust. Tombstone's rows of cabins appear
like a little prisoner-of-war camp, a mini Afghan stalag-luft,
but with great scoff and hot showers.

While CSM Johnstone and his opposite number Pir Ahmed
muster the troops into a hollow square for the photo-parade,
I sit next to Captain Hameed at a table which reflects a solar
glare. We work from left to right, each man marching into a
formal halt and saluting in front of the company commander – an action they've just learnt in Kabul. I take each one's
photograph and record their name, age, Province of origin
and specialist training. Mostly young, small, grubby and
dishevelled, they are not the Afghan tribesmen of Western
stereotype and their appearance belies their heroically beautiful Persian names: Hafizullah (divine guardian), Hakim
Khan (great judge), Jehangir (world ruler). The troops enjoy
the attention, and CSM Johnstone gets some banter going by
getting them to learn his name: 'Sergeant Major Tommy,'
they cry in unison.

Unfortunately there's a serious mismatch between the
names I've recorded and those on Captain Hameed's nomi-
nal roll.

'Where are the other men on your list?' I enquire

'They are absent, they left without permission after the
graduation ceremony in Kabul last month . . . They will not
return,' he says matter-of-factly.

We're left with about thirty men, including NCOs and
officers.

85

Retreating from the fierce sun for tea with Captain Hameed, I broach the subject of what training we might do. He's interested only in driving training and says we can train all those not involved in guarding the perimeter, including, of course, himself. Disappointed by Captain Hameed's lack of enthusiasm and the fact that his company is turning out to be more like a platoon, I decide against discussing the idea of taking a patrol out around the local area. Sipping our tea silently, we chew sweet Panjshiri raisins.

In the innumerable brief pauses between his interpreting for other people, I listen intently to Tamim's gentle voice as he tells me about himself.

'My grandfather's family was from Kandahar, but left for Kabul in the 1960s when my grandfather became a General in King Zahir Shah's army ...'

His family's good fortunes had not survived the last forty years intact.

'My father was employed in the Defence Ministry and was killed by the Mujahideen in 1993, so I fled with my mother and sister to Peshawar. I was fifteen years old. I worked in a matches factory, it was a very difficult time but I worked as hard as I could ...'

Sacrificing any spare time and money available to take English lessons, Tamim eventually returned to Kabul after the fall of the Taliban. Using his knowledge of Pashtu, Dari and English, he got a job interpreting for the US Army, with whom he worked in Kabul and Paktia Province. Money was still tight, however.

'My grandfather was very angry that we had gone to Peshawar and did not forgive us for leaving Kabul. He still refuses to allow us back into his house, so we have to rent an apartment in Macrorayon [vast Soviet housing blocks in Kabul]. My sister is still in school and mother is too ill to work, so I need my wages for the rent and other things.'

I'm touched by his calm honesty. Like me he's in his late twenties, but has already seen a lifetime's worth of trauma. A gentle man, he's sick of violence:

'I'm glad to be away from the Americans. I like them but it was too dangerous. I hope this mission can be safe, soon I want to return to Kabul to marry my girlfriend. The remainder of my wages I'm saving for the celebrations.'

A few days later, I'm sitting in Captain Hameed's office – which now has a metal table and three chairs – drinking the inevitable green tea. Our training has started but is so far limited to some driving with a few of the soldiers, and Captain Hameed instantly dismisses any idea of a patrol whenever I suggest it. He's whinging to Pir Ahmed about the fact that Colonel Shirdil, the battalion commander, has ordered him to remove the photograph of Commander Masood that was fixed to the windscreen of one of HQ Company's Ford Rangers. This has been done to guard against factionalism, which so far seems to be happily absent from the Kandak.

Unannounced, a junior NCO brings in a filthy, sullen soldier and, pulling him by the shoulder, places him before Captain Hameed's desk. The NCO says something to Captain Hameed, who stands up and asks the soldier a question, to which he receives a mumbled reply and a shake of the head. The Captain then harangues the soldier, growing angrier and louder until, advancing around the table, he punches the soldier full in the face. The soldier falls onto his knees and clutches his nose. Kicked in the chest, he falls backwards and crawls for the door, sent on his way by a left and a right kick from Captain Hameed. All this has started and finished so quickly that Tamim can only now interpret the meaning of the conversation. The soldier, Hafizullah, had been found smoking hashish in the lines. Captain Hameed, smoothing his combats, settles back down on his chair and resumes his glass of tea.

Tramping back through the dust to Tombstone, I reflect that the beating I've just witnessed makes me realise how little I know of the ANA from spending a few hours with them each morning. I'm desperate to be properly 'embedded' with the Afghans, to truly get to know them and turn the company into a slick, effective unit. But they're not really interested in doing any serious training, so we end up wasting a lot of time and just drinking gallons of green tea. Perhaps when we start patrolling and go up to FOB Robinson the relationship will feel a bit more meaningful? Each time I return from Shoraback to the clean sterility of Tombstone I feel mildly fraudulent and self-compromised. I'm also annoyed with myself for my enjoyment of the Afghan-free DFAC. As a remedy to this disappointing double-sided existence I spend time with the interpreters as a compromise, a sort of cultural halfway house.

I'm intrigued to be invited by Tamim to take tea after the Friday prayer meeting in Shoraback. The prayers are still under way when I arrive, and I'm about to retreat through the door when Tamim spots me, jumps up and insists that it is appropriate for me to join him. Sliding off my boots, which I've loosened in anticipation, I settle cross-legged next to Tamim as he resumes his devotions. The room has been cleared of all furniture; all that remains is a hollow square of mattresses, full of bodies turned inwards towards a large young man with a full beard and shaven top lip, absorbed in reading silently to himself. This is the mullah, on his weekly visit. Those around him are reading the holy Qur'anic booklets he's brought. They read in whispers, lips moving in vigorous enunciation. Some rock back and forth slightly, in union with the rhythm of the sacred text. At its conclusion the reader kisses the text, holds it to his forehead and replaces it on the stack in the middle of the room, taking another. Some, who cannot read, sit with a friend and listen to a hushed narration. These men have momentarily given up their rank at this prayer meeting. Officers sit by soldiers, with no regard to their distance from the door – unthinkable in any other situation, when a person's status diminishes the closer he is to it. As the prayers end and the tea-drinking begins I feel humbled to be included.

The following day I'm determined to plan a patrol with Captain Hameed. We've done bags of driving training with the small group of guys we get each day and I want to move onto something a bit more meaningful. Surprisingly, perhaps because he's bored with my pestering, he immediately agrees that we should take out a patrol in the local area in a couple of days' time. After this is agreed and we've finished our tea, a small crumpled plastic bag is offered to me by the Captain with a mischievous grin. This is naswar, an ultra-strong mixture of dark pungent tobacco and god-knows-what-else. Its name in Pashtu literally means 'brown'. Having

89

observed him taking it on a daily basis, my curiosity wins over and I accept the little bag, take out a pinch and place it under my tongue. Taking care not to swallow any saliva, I settle on my chair. Within moments my body is beset by a rush of tingling and simultaneously becomes very, very heavy. I sink further into my chair, wanting to roll off and sleep on the floor. I'm briefly amused by this sensation when it's suddenly superseded by a nauseous urge; I struggle off the chair and go outside.

As I leave the office, Major Sayyid, a company commander known as 'the Russian' for his fair complexion, is in the corridor energetically beating a soldier's upturned foot soles. The soldier is held on his back by two assistants. Major Sayyid seems to be expending more energy than necessary due to the fact that his weapon is a broom handle and devoid of the flex appropriate to a whip.

Back in Tombstone, I wander vacuously into the operations room to check for mail. Getting a 'bluey' – an MoD airmail letter free to the families of serving personnel – is absurdly exciting, out of all proportion to its content. A parcel therefore is even more thrilling – pure morale gold dust.

On the TV screen at the back of the operations room a friend's face flashes up. It's Dobson from Sandhurst, a shiny blond grinning face. He's in the Army Air Corps. His brother was in the Scots Guards with me. As I'm drawn to the screen, his image is replaced by a pall of smoke over urban rooftops; this is Basra on the BBC News. His Lynx was shot down. Dobson's dead.

Seconds later the news item changes. Stunned, I check my

post: nothing. I'm very glad to be here; we're detached, far away, which makes his death simple, avoidable. My mourning for Dobson will last for as long as it takes me to turn away from the TV screen and leave the operations room.

Two days later we head over to Shoraback for the patrol. We've got two vehicles; I'm in one with Private Finau – 'Finny', my Fijian driver – and following in the other is CSM Johnstone with Sergeant Stoddart. We've borrowed two extra bodies: one to man the 'Jimpy' (General Purpose Machine Gun) mounted on my wagon and a signaller to monitor the radios.

On our arrival Captain Hameed is in his office wearing flip-flops – not a good 'combat indicator'.

'Captain Leo, let's maybe do the patrol tomorrow,' he says, wincing, clearly intent on having the day off.

At this point, from my recent exposure to the Afghans, I know that 'face' is extremely important. I must get him to change his mind but make it look like his own idea, thus allowing him to avoid appearing work-shy, keep his honour unblemished and save his 'face'.

'I must commend you for your well-judged postponement,' I say, sitting down uneasily on a flimsy metal office chair, encumbered with my body armour and webbing vest, 'but hadn't we better clear this with Colonel Shirdil? He's expecting us to depart immediately, and it would be a shame if your admirable concern about overworking your men were construed as disorganisation or even worse, idleness . . .'

Flip-flops replaced by desert boots, we finally depart after the two hours of chaos required to get three ANA wagons, filled with fuel and each complete with a commander, driver, signaller and as many men as possible (each with an AK) clinging onto the open back, out of the gate.

Thrilled to be out of the cramped monotony of the camp, we bomb around the lunar-desert landscape that surrounds us. It's uninhabited and pancake-flat for miles in all directions, contained only by the summit spikes of the distant Hindu Kush. Kicking up furious dust clouds, we thrash the wagons as fast as possible and practise changing formation on the move, exhilarated by the space, the speed, and the heat.

The Afghans love it. The following day, our rapport is markedly humorous. Even Captain Hameed can't help admitting that he enjoyed it. Interestingly, I felt a little bit of pride when we all parked up outside the headquarters in Camp Bastion and I went inside to tell the operations desk that we were departing; my beard raised numerous eyebrows and I was reminded how glad I was not to be spending my tour in a tent full of computers. I was pleased too that my Afghans could see what a rancid dusty shit-hole Camp Bastion is and that the Brits are living in worse conditions than they are.

I'm also pleased we've got our Afghans out the gate, as our deployment to FOB Robinson is impending. With this departure in mind Colonel Shirdil has ordered that a party be thrown. The Brits provide a PA system (borrowed from the Americans, naturally), the Afghans provide the dancing and the enthusiasm. A Pashtu pop tune is blasted out repeatedly, and a circle of dancers grows. ANA soldiers in grubby green combats and flip-flops move in a rhythmic train, hands in the air with palms raised and backs straight. They kick their heels forward for each step and turn repeatedly inwards then outwards. A cup is produced and balanced on the crown of the finest dancer until with renewed bravado he outdoes himself, the cup tumbles and is passed on . . .

Away from the dancing a football match is played, Brits versus ANA with an interpreter refereeing. The Afghans win on penalties. The ANA doctor, really a male nurse trained thirty years ago in India, is drunk on medicinal spirit and after unsuccessfully picking a fight with a British sergeant, spends the night locked in his own clinic. Later, some wag among the British plays 'I wanna take you to a gay bar' through the PA system. The jest goes unacknowledged by the Afghans and some of their more committed dancers struggle valiantly to maintain a rhythm.

Had they known the song's meaning some of the Afghans might have reflected discreetly that its being played in an ANA camp is not without relevance. Due to the complete absence of any female company, intimate male relation-ships, sometimes homosexual, commonly develop. It is, however, a temporary diversion for the participants while they're deprived of their normal lives rather than anything with long-term meaning. The exact role performed by the tea-boy doting on every ANA officer is consequently a source of endless banter amongst the Brits working with the Afghans.

With the move to FOB Robinson just days ahead, I suggest to Captain Hameed that we take HQ Company to test-fire their rifles. True to form, he suggests an excellent counter-plan which involves staying in camp, definitely drinking tea and probably sleeping. However, Major Sayyid is also present, and says it's a good idea. Captain Hameed agrees, chuckling at my constant enthusiasm for training, which to him seems baffling, misguided and unnecessary. On the range near the camp the soldiers, under the control of CSM Johnstone and Pir Ahmed, fire twenty rounds from their AK47s into wooden targets a hundred metres distant. The troops are keen and are fairly good shots. Before departing, Captain Hameed and I fire off some excess rounds, each taking a turn on the same weapon. I shoot a couple of mags. The AK47 is far louder and has a greater kick than my normal weapon, due to its larger 7.62 cartridge. I hand the AK and a magazine to Captain Hameed. He holds the magazine up to the weapon and struggles with the locking mechanism, approaching it from the wrong end, before clicking it into place. For a former Northern Alliance Mujahid, he's surprisingly unfamiliar with Afghanistan's most common weapon.

The Orders Group the night before the move to FOB Robinson drags on for two hours, mainly because of the interpreting between our commanding officer (a Colonel) and Colonel Shirdil. The 3 Para Patrols (reconnaissance) Platoon will observe the ground five kilometres ahead of us and an American unit will lead our convoy, taking advantage of their aggressive rules of engagement and superior firepower. The appropriately named Sergeant Triggs says they'll happily shoot anyone they don't like the look of with their .50-calibre heavy machine guns and will carry a world's worth of ammunition.

After the main Orders Group I give my own set of orders to my little team in the DFAC: CSM Johnstone, Finny,

Sergeant Stoddart and a signaller who's with us just for the move. I keep it brief, focusing on the route on my map, and what we'll do if we're 'contacted'. We've practised our reaction drills repeatedly so everyone knows it backwards, while also knowing that it'll never be that neat when it's for real.

Exhilarated to be leaving Tombstone, I'm in high spirits as I stitch the ANA badge (crossed swords and delicate Dari script on a green oval) on to my left shirt sleeve, the final piece of preparation before some half-sleep and departure in a couple of hours' time.

CHAPTER 6

Seizing Sangin

May 2006: Helmand Province, Afghanistan

At 0100 we're roaring out of the Tombstone gate in a great column, forty vehicles long, over-revving through the sand, dust billowing into our headlights. I'm thrilled that we're finally leaving after all the waiting around and sluggish preparation. We're fully expecting to be 'contacted' because our impending departure has been a poorly kept secret; everyone, including all the ANA troops, has known about it for the last few days. This anticipation only adds to our excitement.

I'm jammed into the commander's seat (front left-hand side) of my Snatch wagon, which barely accommodates my 6-foot 4-inch frame combined with my body armour, webbing vest, three-litre water-pouch on my back and 9mm pistol strapped to my left leg. I've got my helmet on and my PRR (Personal Role Radio) is strapped onto my left ear. It's for short-distance tactical use, but doesn't work well from inside the vehicle. My rifle is muzzle down, resting between my knees. My own personal GPS (global positioning system) is balanced up against the window on the dashboard in front of me to ensure a continuous signal. Alongside it are my map case and binoculars, which I managed to get in Colchester before deploying. In between Finny and me is a box of a dozen bottles of mineral water which Finny, quietly cheerful as ever, loaded up just before departure. He also had the presence of mind to pop into the DFAC before we left for a last-minute goodies-grab, and has got us two Snickers ice-cream bars each – the most prized of DFAC treasures. I can't face one at the moment, and don't have the heart to suggest that perhaps he might have got something a bit more durable.

It's not long before our convoy comes to a grinding halt: one of the ANA four-tonners is bogged down. Two US Humvees from the rear of the column whizz past to the rescue, bumping effortlessly over the sand that surrounds our dirt track. Twenty minutes later we shudder forward. It's not just the Afghans who get bogged down. Our Snatch wagons are woefully underpowered and ill-suited to cross-country driving. Designed for 'snatching' individuals from a crowd of rioters on Northern Ireland's streets, the inadequacy of the Snatch has been a notorious bugbear for British troops since the invasion of Iraq. Their thin little wheels cut into the patches of sand which cover parts of the road, becoming hopelessly stuck. The British vehicles are repeatedly pulled free by the Americans.

After hitting the tarmac of Route 1 – Afghanistan's national ring-road – the pace quickens and we're relieved to pass through the small town of Gereshk and cross the Helmand River still under the cover of darkness. Shortly, we turn north onto a mud track heading towards the Sangin Valley.

Static again, as we wait for another wagon to be dragged

free, the rising sun keeps us entertained. Tamim and Finny take pictures of each other posing. The expectation of being contacted has, at least momentarily, disappeared. Despite the wasteland appearance, there are occasional signs of life: poppy fields cluster around the irrigation channels that nourish them and lead to small mud-hut farm dwellings. The poppy stalks are now flowerless, brown and shrivelled, having been recently bled of their opium. They'll soon be cut down and have their seeds replanted. A more fleeting spectacle are distant black dots on the horizon – the tents of Koochi shepherds, a nomadic herding tribe of Pashtuns.

Our Snatch wagon has got inch-thick windows for ballistic protection. They don't open, so there's an air-conditioning blower to compensate. Unfortunately ours doesn't work, despite Finny's efforts at checking the fuse. By mid-morning the heat is fierce. I keep the door open to get a through draught, which drops the temperature to the high 40s. Our bodies, baking in body armour, are soon rancid with sweat.

Stopped yet again, we stretch our legs and refill our water satchels from the stack of mineral water bottles between our seats. I share out a four-pack of Del Monte diced peaches, my own DFAC steal. One each for me, Finny, Tamim and the signaller who's with us just for the convoy. Unsated, I sit and wait. Finny dozes. The Snickers ice-cream bars are now liquid.

Finally we crawl forward, and after a total of fourteen hours of stop-start frustration arrive at FOB Robinson to find the US Special Forces team leaving. They're 'bugging out' – making a hurried exit, delighted to be returning to

Kandahar. The little camp, half-familiar to me from the earlier recce, has all (excepting the outer wall) been ripped
down or taken away in an effort to salvage some of the re-
useable fittings. I wouldn't expect such a budgetary con-
straint for the US Special Forces. The Helmand Task Force
headquarters has clearly been unable to negotiate with the
American command to keep this crucial infrastructure in
place, which means we'll be sleeping in the sand. A new
watchtower, completed just days previously, lists precariously against the perimeter, its legs sheared off. All that
remains is a wooden shack and a couple of metal shipping
containers, doors open, spilling out crushed boxes of American rations. The deep sand is cluttered with rubbish – food
packaging, Coke cans, metal ammunition boxes and hundreds of spent .50-calibre brass cases. The Special Forces
team, muscular and bearded, jubilantly mount up onto
their Humvees, adjust their sunglasses and settle behind
their weapons. As they leave the gate they test-fire their
weapons into the side of the road, and a frantic rattling
echoes up the valley.

We 'bivi-up' at the corners of the perimeter, stretching our
plastic ponchos between the earthen perimeter wall and the
sand and foraging among the remnants of the smashed-up
camp for sheets of plywood on which to unroll our sleeping
bags. The left-over ammo boxes make excellent seats and
mini-tables. The challenge of creating a little living space has
refreshed our enthusiasm after the tedium of the convoy and
the disappointment of finding the camp in a shit state. The
ANA are adjacent to us, in another large perimeter towards
the river. Their Kandak HQ is in a walled compound with

brick rooms and they live in their watchtowers, so they're better off than we are.

The sun disappears beyond the Helmand River below us, but we're too absorbed in our new activity to take photos. We 'stag on' – mount guard – in pairs next to our bivi positions. Two hours each in rotation, spent staring into the night through the green glow of a Common Weapon Sight (night-viewing aid). We've got one in our team. Each man should really have night-vision goggles (NVGs) but the kit shortage has not yet been sorted. Erratically the night's silence is smashed by the pounding, ear-splitting boom of artillery, the ANA firing their howitzers at Taliban targets – maybe real, probably imagined.

Coming off my second stag as dawn breaks, I tumble exhausted onto my dust-laden sleeping bag. I'm woken about an hour later by a signaller from HQ: there's something on. The officers and senior NCOs gather round our Colonel's vehicle. An order has come from Helmand Task Force headquarters: we are to 'seize Sangin and re-establish governance'. The town is apparently overrun with Taliban; we must immediately carry out a planned attack, kill or disperse any Taliban, and allow the Afghan authorities to govern. Full details will follow at a bigger Orders Group in two hours. 'Holy shit!' I think, taking in the Colonel's words. It's incredibly sudden and unexpected but I'm game!

Electrified, I pace back to our bivi position and relay the message to CSM Johnstone, Finny and Sergeant Stoddart. They accept it without question. Frantic with excitement we start cramming our two Snatch wagons with ammunition, water and rations scavenged from the American leftovers.

We need a third wagon, so Sergeant Stoddart heads off to the ANA compound to see what he can find. As I make my way over to the O-group my stomach swirls with adrenalin.

'Fucking hell!' I think. 'This is it for real, a deliberate attack!'

The Orders Group takes place in the shade of a parachute canopy suspended from the mud walls of the American Training Team's compound. The officers and some senior NCOs of the British mentoring team are crowded around a map pinned to the mud wall. Its scale is 1:10,000, so individual buildings can be seen. I got my copy while ADC, which is just as well because we're short of these decent large-scale maps. Mixed in with us is the American training team: a dozen laconic National Guardsmen, who seem tired but utterly reliable. They're commanded by an unexcited but very willing black Colonel with powerful rounded shoulders and big hands. Some of these guys are probably nine months into their one-year tour, so they've seen it all before. It's their Kandak coming into town with us: the Heratis I met during the Commander's recce. We're meant to have relieved them, but they're better equipped and more prepared than our Kandak, which will stay at the FOB and guard the perimeter. The Kandak commander is the last to arrive. He's late, but only because he was the last to be told what's happening. He's a neat little Herati with a slight goatee beard and Mongol eyes. His second-in-command is with him, a suave Pashtun with his green beret clinging rakishly to his head.

Before this audience the Colonel sets out his plan of attack. He's what he himself would call 'a strapping cove', a broad-chested rugby player with sensible good looks who speaks with the confident ease of a man not interested in details. We'll enter the town from the east, approaching along a dry riverbed. The 3 Para Patrols Platoon (still here from yesterday) will guide the advance. The British teams will take an ANA company each, the order of march being 3 Company, 2 Company then 1 Company (with my team).

The Colonel's command group will be located just behind the lead company at all times. Half of the US team will go directly to the southern end of the town to block any enemy movement and be a diversion, the other half will travel in front of the lead company in order to provide extra firepower. (They've got .50-calibre machine guns on their Humvees, which pack more than twice the punch of a normal rifle.) We'll head for the District Chief's compound, as that's the seat of local government. We don't know where that is exactly; I mark three possible locations on my map. Apart from the fact that the town is apparently being over-run with Taliban, we've no more real information on the enemy.

The Colonel takes questions. One officer looks stricken.

'We're not equipped for this. We don't have night-vision goggles, or enough vehicles . . . We're a training team, this is not our job.'

'Don't be silly, it's perfectly within our means,' replies the Colonel, unmoved.

I agree with the Colonel. Let's do it! We could be better prepared and equipped but so what? This is a *real* deliberate, pre-planned attack. It's the most exciting thing that could possibly happen, and I'm up for it!

Lastly, the Colonel says our rules of engagement have been changed to war-fighting mode. This means that we can kill anyone we deem to be the enemy without them having to shoot at us first. Identifying the enemy may be tricky – the Taliban aren't going to be wearing uniforms – but common sense must prevail. The same officer again stands and asks for confirmation of whether this has been made officially legal by the Helmand Task Force headquarters. A hush falls on our group. This is almost insubordination, questioning the veracity of a commanding officer's orders.

The Colonel points at him with a karate-chop hand. 'Fucking shut up and get on with it.'

With only minutes to go before we have to meet up with our ANA company, I scurry back to our vehicles. I'm up for it, really up for it! I know we're doing the whole thing on a wing and a prayer but that just makes it more intoxicating; anything could happen! I also love the 're-establish governance' bit. It's unclear exactly how we'll do this after seizing control of the town but I'm inherently comfortable with the notion of just 'cracking on' and exhilarated by the total uncertainty, reality and immediacy of this moment.

I have barely two minutes to give orders to my team. With cardboard tags hastily torn from a ration-pack box, I show them how the plan will work on my map. I tell them what our mission is, cover medical casualty evacuation (Sergeant Stoddart will apply first aid after which a helicopter should come if it's serious) and tell them about the war-fighting rules of engagement. They all accept this without question, quietly nodding. We mount up, now with a third vehicle – Stoddy has come up trumps with his scrounging. He's found a dented old ANA wagon, essentially a Ford pick-up truck spray-painted beige. It's hardly twenty-first-century war-fighting kit, but it's better than nothing.

Amid a chaos of dust and vehicles we meet Number 1 Company. They're in a column of eight pick-ups. I lead our three wagons to the front, ahead of the two belonging to the Kandak commander. He's oddly placed here; we're starting off as the reserve company at the rear, surely he should be further forward? From one of the trucks Hindi film music blares, its sweet soprano blurred by the volume. The Afghan soldiers clambering into their pick-up trucks shout excitedly at one another, thrilled by the sudden break in their mundane routine of watchtower duty. Wearing only berets or camouflage caps rather than helmets, without body armour and clutching their AKs, they seem sprightly compared to us, swaddled in cumbersome, hot but potentially life-saving personal equipment.

The company commander, Captain Birialay, steps forward. A smiling, fleshy-faced Pashtun from Jalalabad, he speaks Urdu and is delighted at my response in the same language. He's happy with the plan, or rather, happy to know it vaguely, unconcerned about its merits. He's a charming and jovial combination of careless optimism and fatalism, both enabled by a complete submission to divine providence. All will be well, 'insh'allah' – if God wills it.

Our convoy crawls through the FOB gate and then lurches forward, as if suddenly released, becoming a dusty snake of racing vehicles, all trying to keep up. I'm chasing the ANA wagons of Number 2 Company and being chased by Sergeant Stoddart and CSM Johnstone. The ANA following us keep dropping back. We're forced to pause, swearing and keeping one eye on the distant rising dust plume of the convoy ahead. The whole town will know we're coming at this rate. We're doing a big loop far into the hills to the northeast, for at least a dozen kilometres, to avoid being seen before we enter the town from the east, but we can hardly be going unnoticed . . .

Shortly before the dry riverbed that leads into town and behind a high, ragged ridge, the convoy stops. I get a quick brief from the Colonel: I'm to occupy the ridge to our front, for use as a helicopter landing site in case we take casualties that need evacuation. I'm also to be ready to move forward 'to echelon through' if the enemy opposition is strong. We get a section of eight Artillery soldiers to strengthen our team; with no space in our two Snatch, they pile into the back of Stoddy's knackered ANA wagon. I relay these orders to the Kandak Commander and Captain Birialay from the bonnet of the Commander's pick-up. From the map my eye is caught by the gaudy plastic flowers and red velvet covering the Commander's dashboard. A cluster of blue-bead charms dangle from the rear-view mirror, a ready defence against the evil eye.

Up on the ridge we spread out, observing in all directions in a defensive posture. We can see the centre of town about five kilometres away, but it's pretty miniature at this range, a low brown jumble of flat-roofed houses and mud compounds with the odd big house jutting up, clad in green and blue tiles. On its left-hand side, to the west, the brown drab merges into a shock of vivid green. This is the fertile ribbon accompanying the swollen Helmand River as it winds south.

From up here it looks peaceful, but really we're too far away to tell. I'd like to move further down to get a closer look but our priority is to secure the helicopter landing site until called forward.

Using my GPS I get a ten-figure grid reference of a our location and send it on the radio back to 'zero', our head-quarters in FOB Robinson. We've got a secure high-frequency radio, part of the Army's new digital system, and it's working reasonably well so far. I've got a signaller in the back with the set, with a headset passed through to me in the front so we can both use it. The antenna has to poke through the hatch used by the top-cover bods as there's not one built into the vehicle itself. For a better signal, if we're stationary we put the set up on the roof. Sitting in my wagon I can see the ANA are still in good spirits; Capt Birialay's team is getting a brew on with a kerosene burner and a big steel teapot.

The radio crackles semi-coherent messages; it's the other companies talking to one another as they move into the town. From among this burble a terse voice is suddenly clear:

'Hello zero this is four one alpha ... Contact wait out ...'

'Fuck, it's kicked off,' I exclaim, keeping the headset jammed to my ear.

I order all engines turned off. The Hindi music drifting from the company commander's vehicle continues a defiant solo until I stifle that too. In the silence we wait for details. I'm half hoping it's a false alarm, half hoping something sig-nificant enough has occurred so that we too can get involved. The outcome is inconclusive: shots have been fired in both directions, but there's no enemy to be seen so it's not a deci-sive engagement. Accepting Captain Birialay's offer of tea I leave the signaller to man the radio and join him by his pick-up. I don't protest when the Hindi music restarts.

Sipping my tea, I notice that the Kandak commander, bored with hanging around, has headed off into the dry riverbed to our front with his two vehicles. From the mud-walled compound that he's just passed small figures are emerging and moving hurriedly to the east away from the town. They're clearly running away. I hope that we're not watching the first refugees from Sangin since the Soviet war of the 1980s.

Tea unfinished, we're ordered over the radio to move towards the town, staying on the high ground. We make a rapid descent into the dry riverbed and head for the next ridge. The track leading up is precipitous and fragmented. Finny grinds the gears and we crawl upwards, the Snatch engine straining frantically. The rear wheels begin to slide downhill, to our left. 'Top cover down!' I shout, anticipating a roll, the front wheels now also moving sideways. With Finny keeping the revs going the wheels finally bite and we remain upright, lurching precariously forward.

At the top of the ridge, we're surrounded by apparently empty mud-walled compounds, marking the start of the southern end of the town. These compounds are tight-knit and high-walled: easy cover for anyone approaching and not an ideal place for us to be. Entering a large broken-down compound, we get our vehicles in an awkward all-round defence and observe in all directions. The ANA follow on and spread out into the compounds around us.

I put my wagon behind a high wall, stand on the bonnet and scan the town with my binoculars. I can just about make out the main road in Sangin, the 611, running north into the bazaar, which seems to be marked by a tall blue building; perhaps that's the objective. I can't see any people but really I'm still too far away and the light is fading into dusk. Even so, it's still warm and we're dehydrated from sweating perpetually into our body armour and helmets. Finny hands me a big bottle of mineral water. Crouching on the bonnet, I take off my boiling helmet, rub my temples and drain the whole bottle straight down.

Shots crackle to our immediate left . . .

'FUCK! Get down!' I shout, tumbling off the bonnet and grabbing the radio handset dangling above my seat.

'Hello zero this is four one charlie contact wait out . . .' All I want is to know what's happening.

'Get yer helmet on, sir,' CSM Johnstone calmly shouts from his wagon. Having jammed my helmet on, I make a crouched run to the ruined wall to the left, throw myself over and crawl round a pile of bricks to see half a dozen ANA full of panicked fervour crouching and shouting, pointing their AKs at the next compound.

'Kya ho gaya hai . . . kya hua,' I shout, asking what has happened, but my Urdu makes no impression on them. I can't tell if we've been shot at or if the ANA were the ones shooting. Tamim's still in the wagon and I can't understand their Dari. There's nobody to be seen in the compound ahead and the ANA are now shouting at one another, getting stressed. We need to get out of these compounds and off this hillside. With a shout and a wave of my arm – standing in for a language we all understand – I tell the ANA soldiers, 'Let's go!'

In the gathering darkness we wind our way down towards

the main road through deserted, narrow lanes between high mud walls. This is *really* not a good place to be. Eventually the ground levels off, we hit a bigger road and are delighted to see a pair of Humvees parked up; this must be route 611 that runs north into town and the Americans must be the southern block, still in place. The black Colonel emerges and with a friendly 'How y'all doin?' points us in the direction of the British command group. They're at the petrol station in the middle of the bazaar, straight up the road. Leaving the ANA with the Humvees I go with my team to get orders. We have to give Stoddy a push to get started: his ANA cast-off wagon is just about dead.

At the Colonel's vehicle I neck another whole bottle of water. Little speakers rigged up on the roll bars crackle out a Dire Straits song. With the other company commanders I compare notes – there was some shooting when the lead company entered the town but it's uncertain who initiated it; it may have been the ANA shooting at civilians and/or Taliban, or vice versa. Certainly it's not been a decisive engagement and if the Taliban were occupying the town they've disappeared pretty sharply. Perhaps whoever supplied the original intelligence to the Helmand Task Force headquarters was misinformed, or deliberately misinformed us? Anyway an eleven-year-old boy was killed, shot in the head, probably by the ANA or the ANP (Afghan National Police), who had also joined the lead company. Nevertheless the Colonel is in good spirits: we've achieved our objective, Sangin has been seized, we're in the middle of town and we've got the run of the place. Again due to our lack of intelligence it's still unclear exactly where the 'District Centre' is, but the priority for now is to secure the town overnight. My team is to occupy the main police station on route 611 at the southern end of the town, Number 2 Company is to occupy the main bazaar and 3 Company is to watch over the bazaar from the ridge to the south-east (towards where we've just been). I leave the Orders Group and head back to my team on the main route. As the Dire Straits song fades, it occurs to me that I prefer the Hindi music.

The police station is easy to find, a high mud-walled compound with twin turrets at the entrance. A Soviet tank, a rusted trophy, serves as seating for a gaggle of men wearing dark shawls and clutching AKs who wave us in. The Kandak commander is already here and we're expected. The courtyard, though very broad, is half full with a cluster of old Soviet armoured vehicles. With a frightful gnashing of gears we squeeze our Snatch wagons in, facing them towards the gate in case we need to leave suddenly. The ANA follow us in.

Exhausted, our team spills from the back of the wagons. CSM Johnstone says he'll get some guys on the walls of the compound and get a 'stag' routine going. I need to find the Kandak commander to make sure he's happy with the overnight plan. Tamim reckons he's next door with the Chief of Police. Shattered, wretched with filth and stewed in stale sweat, I walk with Tamim through to the other half of the police station, an inner compound separated by a wall.

A clump of willows half-masks a low yellow light besieged by moths. I stoop under their branches and on righting myself see a multitude of richly bearded faces sitting around the edges of an inner square of dark red carpets. All are reclining, most with cushions, sipping tea. A small fountain to the rear trickles softly, beneath boughs of violet-pink blossom. The low murmur of voices pauses slightly on my arrival and then continues as I take off my boots and walk onto the carpet to greet the Kandak commander. He gestures me to sit. I put down my rifle, put my helmet on top and unbuckle my webbing vest. Wrenching open my body armour, a wave of heat rushes up from my slimy sweat-sodden shirt. Reclining cross-legged on a cushion, I heave a sigh of blissful relief. Bathed in soft light, we sip tea and crunch the white sugary sweets put in front of us, gobbling more as our hunger ignites. I'm stunned that such an exquisite little pleasure garden can exist here, a sanctuary of calm so closely adjacent to filth and chaos. Two courtyards in the same compound, each the perfect opposite of the other. This is Afghanistan's seductive, tragic paradox: beauty among brutality, terrible violence amid peerless hospitality.

The Kandak commander is flanked by his second-in-command and Captain Birialay. Before him, reclining in the middle of the carpets, is a great bear of a man swaddled in a black *shalwar qamiz* and waistcoat, leaning back, hands behind his head. This can only be the Chief of Police. Deep-set eyes blackened with kohl shine from his big beefy face. His hands nudge his jewelled prayer cap forward over thick black curls. He chats away with the Kandak commander, Tamim providing an intermittent interpretation; he says he needs more police and more weapons. He's asking for help to secure the police station.

I confirm with the Kandak commander that he's happy with the overnight plan and ask what he intends to do tomorrow. He just gives a 'we'll see' upwards turn of his head and resumes his chat with the Chief of Police. Shortly they both stand, then leave with Captain Birialay, to check on their men in the other parts of town. I briefly discuss the day's events with the Kandak second-in-command, and he tells me that the much-sought District Centre is just up the road at the top of the bazaar, near the river. Soon, he quietly unfolds his blanket, and offers me one. I decline and, keen to ensure that my team is happy, return to my wagon.

Finny is fast asleep in his seat. Only the signaller is awake, monitoring the radio next to two slumbering bodies. Beside the two other wagons at the foot of the wall, sleeping bodies are curled on ponchos spread out on the ground. The guards on the wall tops move slightly, silhouetted by the rising moonlight. I should sleep in my seat, in the front of my vehicle, where I can be easily found in an emergency, but I want really to accept the second-in-command's kind offer. After telling the signaller where I'll be, I return with Tamim to the other courtyard and stretch out beneath a pestilent blanket next to a row of still bodies. Under brilliant stars, I plummet into sleep, unbothered by the fluttering of moths' wings about my face.

Just before dawn the Afghans around me quickly fold their blankets and wash briskly in the fountain. I make my way to the front gate and climb up one of the watchtowers to survey the town, still silent and deserted, as it slowly emerges in the dawn's orange light. Turning, I look back across to the police station. The two courtyards lie side by side, one sprouting willow boughs and cherry blossom, the other a tangled mass of decaying tank hulls, pick-up trucks and filth.

A couple of hours later we make our way in convoy back

up to the middle of the bazaar. It's now full of people and normal daily life seems to be going ahead uninterrupted. On the Colonel's orders, we depart in convoy with the Americans and the ANA for FOB Robinson, leaving Sangin as it was before, in the charge of the police.

CHAPTER 7

The District Centre

Back in FOB Robinson we're dazed but happy, as the adrenalin and excitement of the last couple of days is superseded by relief and good humour. CSM Johnstone takes the piss out of Stoddy and his 'ANA taxi' and joshes Finny for nearly rolling the wagon. 'That was bonkers,' declares Stoddy, 'but we came through it – thank fuck!' Laughing, we get stuck into an 'admin phase': cleaning out our vehicles and restocking them with water and rations. We try to improve our rough shelters, seeking respite from the savage dust; a westerly wind races through the FOB and whips it up, throwing it into our little corner. CSM Johnstone and Stoddy peg their poncho sheets firmly to the ground, making mini-tents.

Finny gives up. 'I'd rather sleep in the wagon, boss, where I normally do.'

I erect a sheet of plywood against the perimeter wall as a windbreak and stretch my poncho over the top. Inside I put my issued mosquito net over my sleeping bag and arrange two metal tins, empty mortar containers, as a seat. With some more dedicated pilfering among the piles of American detritus I find a plywood box, which, when stood upright, makes an excellent wardrobe. The addition of some four-inch nails allows the convenient dust-free stowage of my weapon and headgear. Above all of this we string up a camouflage net of beige nylon foliage to provide shade and cover when we're on stag at night.

While the wind brings dust, a lucky gust has also brought a fleeting aroma of baking bread. Our neighbour on the perimeter, in the shack next to us, is the baker. Captivated by the scent, and offering salaams, I venture in. Sitting cross-legged on the lip of the tandoor that descends deep into the ground, the baker beams up a smile, asks his assistant to get some tea ready, and continues his working rhythm. On a low platform to his left he rolls a fist of dough into a flat oval, folds in the margins, prongs the surface with his arched fingers, stretches it onto a damp cushion and, leaning forward into the glowing tandoor, plants it onto the hot oven wall. Then, with a long steel rod in each hand, he again leans in, and skewers and carries out a fragrant naan, freshly baked after three or four minutes on the oven wall. His assistant takes the hot flat breads as they arrive in a steady rhythm, stacking them neatly by the door. The cycle continues until at least forty naan are in delectable warm lines. Resting his tools, the baker, Mohammad Qasim, wipes his glistening face and, handing me a bread, says I'm most welcome. He's a Pashtun, but having spent time across the Pakistan border in Quetta he's happy to speak Urdu. He has an earnest, wholesome and very cheerful face. Over tea he tells me that he's from Gereshk and has been employed by the Americans here for the last few months.

'I'm glad of the work, Captain Sahib, I make more money working here than in Gereshk, but the contract is just until the end of the month.'

The bread he makes feeds the security guards that the American Special Forces employed to guard the camp; they're leaving shortly, now that the American Special Forces have gone. With their departure Mohammad's contract will finish. As I bid him farewell he shakes my hand in both of his; they are soft but powerful.

'Perhaps you British might employ me?' he asks, still smiling.

'I'll ask my boss, but to be honest . . . we're not quite organised yet,' I reply glumly.

I know that, not having had the means to prevent the guts of the camp from being ripped out, it's rather unlikely that the Quartermaster in Helmand Task Force headquarters is going to stump up the cash to continue the loyal baker's contract.

The naan makes an ideal addition to our early evening meal. Stoddy's game but CSM Johnstone declines – if I'm eating local food he'd better not is his reckoning, so that we're not both ill at the same time. Under the camouflage net we sit on ammo tins and break out MREs – Meals Ready to Eat, American rations. Opening the brown plastic packet is like enjoying a bit of anonymous post. The main menu is printed on the outside but the little sundries always vary. What I covet most is peanut M&Ms, which sadly don't appear this time. I enjoy Mexican fajitas garnished with bright yellow cheese, squeezed from its packet like toxic toothpaste. CSM Johnstone has found some four-packs of

Del Monte tinned fruit in the American storage containers. I eat the diced pears, he tucks into the peaches, observing that they probably all taste the same anyway.

At about 1800 we're called together for an Orders Group – it's a 'well done' from the Colonel. He's pleased with the way it went in town. He goes on for a bit too long and we're shifting uncomfortably on our ammo tins and other makeshift seats when a signaller arrives with a scrap of paper. The Colonel reads it and digests it briefly before telling us its content. It's an order from Helmand Task Force headquarters: the police station in Sangin is under threat from a large Taliban force approaching the town, and we need to go back in and secure it. He'll send an ANA company and one British team with it – any volunteers?

My hand is straight up. I'm still up for it; besides, my team knows the police station and I'd much rather be out there in town than 'stagging on' in this dusty shit-hole of a camp. He agrees and, as the rest of the group disperses, we sort out the ORBAT (Order of Battle: who's doing what job). I'll take my team, in two Snatch wagons, and the same ANA company as last time. The Colonel will escort us in with his two vehicles. We'll also take with us the British platoon who came in yesterday by helicopter when the Helmand Task Force HQ realised that during the operation to seize the town there were no British troops left in the FOB. Our ANA battalion is, probably correctly, not yet trusted to hold the base alone.

In darkness, our convoy departs. I'm leading, with the ANA just behind me followed by the British platoon and then the Colonel's group. We're trying to do it in complete blackness, using night-vision goggles which we've borrowed at the last minute just before going out of the gate from the Artillery guys manning the 105mm light guns. They're damned tricky to use, however, and Finny's really struggling to see anything at all. We move slowly, straining to make out the road, relying on our top-cover blokes to help out. After I fail to see our turn-off in a dry riverbed, forcing the entire convoy to do a U-turn, the Colonel orders us over the radio to sack the goggles and get a move on with white light. Headlights blazing, we race to the police station.

On arrival I leave CSM Johnstone and Tamim with Captain Birialay to give the British platoon a hand manning the compound, and go with the Kandak commander and some of Number 1 Company up to an over-watch position on a ridge to the south-east, near our route of the previous evening.

Up on the hill, we park up close to the Kandak commander, who's spread his men out. In my wagon I've got a signaller and top-cover bloke with Finny driving as usual. We take turns doing one hour standing up in the top-cover hatch and staring down into the town, which is completely dark but for a few compounds, including the police station, illuminated by their own generators. Nearer to us on the eastern side of town are silhouetted four squat tower-like houses in large compounds, perhaps the product of the narco-affluence that Sangin must possess as a trading post for the opium industry, where growers sell raw opiate gum to refiners and transporters. After my stag I sleep on the bonnet, reclining onto the windscreen, my rifle in my lap. It's a quiet night apart from an occasional rustling at the top of the wagon – Finny on stag, extracting a few nuts from his pocket.

Coming off the hill just after sun-up we meet the British Colonel in the police station. He's come for a meeting with the Chief of Police and the District Chief to try to find out what exactly is going on in Sangin.

Making our way through to the courtyard where I slept two nights previously, we find the Kandak commander and the Chief of Police breakfasting on a veranda abutting the outside wall. The British Colonel exchanges a brief 'salaam alaykum' and sits next to the Kandak commander, opposite the Chief of Police. I'm further down, next to Captain Biri-alay, with Tamim on my left. The rest of the space is taken by the police: beautiful thugs, non-uniformed, in brown and blue *shalwar qamiz*, shawls and jewelled caps, with AKs by their sides. We're cross-legged on a long carpet on which is stretched an elongated white cotton sheet. A gangly youth circulates with a large stack of naan on his left shoulder and places one in front of each person. Tea from a big boiling kettle follows in little glasses. The fresh naan combined with the hot sweet tea is especially delicious after the night up on the hill.

The Chief of Police immediately asks the British Colonel for more weapons and men. His force is insufficient, he says, to protect the town from the Taliban. The Colonel says he has no weapons to hand out, but that we'll make a plan to protect the town that'll involve the ANA. Shortly, another man joins the group, sitting down to the right of the Police Chief. A big man with a white *shalwar qamiz* and faded scarlet prayer cap, hawk-nosed and with long elegant moustaches combed into a great red-black beard, this is the District Chief, Haji Khan Mohammed, the Governor's representative in Sangin. He greets the Chief of Police in the traditional Pashtun manner, an extended series of reciprocal good wishes and repetitive polite questions: 'How are you? Are you well? Don't be tired, how are you? Be healthy . . .' Despite the greeting the two men show no real warmth for one another. The British Colonel asks him what is happening in Sangin. The District Chief rolls up a bit of naan, pops it into his mouth, chews deliberately, swallows it with a slurp of tea and says that perhaps it would be best if the Colonel came to the District Centre where he can be his guest and they can talk at length more comfortably. As he says this, the Chief of Police is silent and stony faced. The only thing that's clear about these two is that they dislike each other. I know that we're seeing only the tip of a very complex situation. The Colonel agrees and says we'll go there with him now.

Jumping into our wagons, we follow the District Chief to his compound. Bumping along the pot-holed road we chase his Toyota Land Cruiser, chock-full of his militia-men clinging onto the back. The bazaar, a continuous line of small shop fronts crammed together, right up against the road, is open and busy. Shop owners sit cross-legged, surrounded by produce: vegetables, meat, bread, shoes, clothes, pots and pans, umbrellas, bicycles . . . Those in the bazaar, dark and bearded, gaze at us passively. Toyota Corolla estate cars full of passengers edge to the roadside to let us pass. At a fork we turn left and head west towards the river. Out of the bazaar, buildings suddenly mingle with lush orchards, vivid green wheat fields and little farmsteads. Passing over a small bridge and along a track with tall trees on either side, we arrive at the long-sought-for District Centre: a big flat-roofed one-storey building, whitewashed and surrounded by fertile gardens. There's a veranda at its front with big square columns decorated with green and blue paint in a diamond pattern. A gang of militia men wave us in and we swiftly dismount. The Colonel, Tamim and I go with the District Chief into his small reception room, the *hijra*, the only contents of which are a well-worn dark carpet and some long cylindrical cushions.

As we sip our tea, the Colonel asks the Chief about the Taliban: where are they? The Chief says they come from villages like Jushalay, north of Sangin, and that he can help us find them. However, it's not really the Taliban that he wants to talk about.

'Colonel, the real problem in Sangin is the police. They're corrupt and violent. They harass and abuse the population and extort money from them.'

'Why don't you stop this?' the Colonel asks. 'You're the District Chief.'

'It would only lead to more bloodshed. The Chief of Police is the real problem. He himself is a criminal and a murderer – he killed a fourteen-year-old boy. But I cannot control him. If I try to, he'll start a feud which I couldn't win . . .'

The Colonel suggests a Shura, a meeting, to allow the elders of Sangin to discuss what's been happening and what should be done about it. They could also discuss the idea for a new 'auxiliary police force' that has been proposed, apparently by the Governor's office. The Chief agrees to call the elders together for the following morning. He also assures the Colonel disinterestedly that he's heard about the new police idea and, quickly moving on, suggests a more immediate solution to the problem.

'Colonel, if your troops were to stay here and patrol the town, the police would not be able to harass the civilians . . .'

The Colonel, with a karate chop of the hand, is decisive. 'You'll have troops here by this afternoon with Captain Docherty. My soldiers and the ANA will be all over the bazaar, we'll dominate this town.'

Smiling, he looks askance at me. 'Happy with that, Leo?'

'Delighted, sir. This place has got "platoon house" written all over it.'

As the Colonel bids farewell to the Chief I bound up a set of stone steps onto the roof of the District Centre. I quickly scan a 360; I've got excellent arcs of view all round. I can see most of the town, the other side of the Sangin valley, and northward up the Helmand River. The dry riverbed used as the axis of advance during our first entry into town joins the river basin from the east and we're on the corner of land between the two. There's a taller building under construction next door on the northern side, which would make an excellent observation post. The dry riverbed would make a good helicopter landing site and could be easily covered by troops on the roof of the new building. Overall it seems like an ideal place from which to conduct patrols.

As I descend from the roof, shiny red fruits in a tree catch my eye. 'Oh my God, pomegranates!'

Rejoicing inwardly, I mount up and our convoy departs, heading back to FOB Robinson.

Back at the base it becomes apparent that getting hold of sufficient Afghan troops to 'dominate' Sangin is going to be a problem. The Herati Kandak, who we've used on our two previous forays into town, are now demanding to be released to return to Herat. We came to the FOB in the first place in order to relieve them, so their demand is hardly unreasonable. Unfortunately the Kandak we brought with us is 60 per cent under strength. They've got a lot of men away on leave but the real problem is the desertion that occurred after they left Kabul Military Training Centre. The remainder totals fewer than two hundred men, all of whom are supposedly occupied with manning the watchtowers around FOB Robinson and guarding the vast perimeter.

With the British second-in-command, a Major, I go to see Colonel Shirdil in the Kandak headquarters – a courtyard busy with ANA vehicles and rubbish, enclosed by low brick buildings. Each of the five companies within the Kandak has an office here, as does Colonel Shirdil; it doubles up as his sleeping quarters. Sitting on his bed, the Major requests that some men are made available, to help man the platoon house.

Colonel Shirdil immediately launches into a lengthy complaint. 'Where are the heavy weapons I was promised before coming to Sangin? I can only just guard the perimeter, I haven't enough men to send any into town . . .'

His big square head nods up and down almost in rhythm with his speech, accompanied by his long hands: the right slapping the palm of the left. After an agitated few minutes he tails off into silence, white reservoirs of saliva having gathered at the corners of his mouth. Awkwardly we drink our tea.

'Maybe if I just took one or two men, it could be like a recce,' I suggest.

This would allow Shirdil to be seen to be making a clever

move, while also agreeing to our request and consequently saving face. Colonel Shirdil turns to speak to his second-in-command and, with a mute nod of his head, agrees. I'm hoping that it will snowball a little and, one officer having been given the go-ahead, he'll bring a few spare soldiers with him.

Emerging from Shirdil's room, I meet Captain Hameed outside the HQ Company office.

'Where have you been, Captain Leo?' he asks.

'In Sangin, Hameed Jaan [Dear Hameed]. In fact why don't you come back into town with me? Colonel Shirdil has ordered that one officer should come along.'

As Tamim interprets my response, the Captain rolls his eyes, half amused at my naive optimism. I clearly don't realise how impossible that would be.

'Sadly, Captain Leo, I'm far too busy. A spare officer will be found to come with you.'

Captain Ahmed, a softly spoken Pashtun, is the spare officer. He meets me with a pick-up and five ANA soldiers, including Javed, a soldier whom I know from HQ Company. On the way out of the FOB we throw boxes of halal rations, unappealing biriyani packed in India, into the back of their pick-up. I've got a small team in one Snatch: a signaller – Lance Corporal Bow – and a top-cover bloke, with Finny driving as usual. We're taking the British platoon to provide the manpower; everyone else is required to guard the perimeter of our compound in case there's another full-frontal attack like the one in March. For the third time in as many days we bump along the pot-holed 611 back into town.

At the District Centre, the British platoon occupy the unfinished building. My team with the ANA occupy a small room opposite the Chief's *hijra*. We park the Snatch wagon close to the building and man the radio. Having done a radio check to the FOB, I'm eager to patrol into town before sunset.

I put Javed at the front and Captain Ahmed just behind me. We're leading two sections – eight-man teams – from the British platoon. The third section of the platoon will stay at the District Centre as a Quick Reaction Force, which I can call on the radio carried by Lance Corporal Bow. The District Centre would be left empty but that's not a worry as it's crawling with the Chief's militia.

As we make our way into the dry riverbed running east towards the 611 and the top of the bazaar, I realise that we're the first foot patrol that Sangin has seen in a very long time. The Canadians came through in their armoured vehicles and the US special forces raced through in their Humvees, but this is the first fully dismounted patrolling that's been done by Coalition forces.

We're without headdress or sunglasses. I've got my para helmet clipped with a karabiner to the rear right-hand side of my webbing vest. My pouches contain five magazines of 30 rounds each (there's one fitted on my rifle), two bandoliers of 5.56 ammunition (300 rounds), two smoke grenades, a red phosphorus grenade and a high-explosive grenade. In addition to this, in my left chest pocket I've two super-absorbent dressings and a morphine injector, marked with a big 'M' on the outside of the pouch. In my right chest pocket I have my GPS and spare batteries for my radio, which is clipped onto my left shoulder with the headset jammed to my left ear, held on by an elastic strap over my forehead. My vest also has flat zipped pockets on the front, holding a map and a second magazine for my 9mm pistol, which hangs down my right leg in a green canvas holster. The black plastic one that I got in Kandahar broke the night before we left Tombstone so Jim, my bunk-bed neighbour, gave me his, angry that dealing with the interpreters' pay and other staff work in Camp Tombstone was not going to give him a reason to wear a combat holster.

All of this, with my three-litre water pouch, body armour, rifle and pistol, weighs easily about twenty kilograms, a hot and uncomfortable but manageable burden. Lance Corporal Bow stoically carries a good deal more than twenty kilos with his HF radio set. We've removed our sunglasses to allow us to look people in the eye and appear less threatening, but it's perhaps a meaningless improvement to a bunch of 'feringhees' (white people) wandering around like sweaty Robocops.

We walk up the dry riverbed in staggered file, with men on alternate sides. Approaching a bridge that takes the 611 over the riverbed we come into a poultry market. Squawking beady-eyed white chickens are stacked up in wire-mesh crates on rickety stalls of wooden poles and plastic sheeting. Ascending to the main road, we move south onto the main bazaar. It's six o'clock and the men of Sangin are doing their evening shopping. Their response to our presence is discreetly curious and sometimes friendly. I greet those whose eyes I meet in Pashtu – 'Staray mashay' ('May you not be tired') – and a restrained wave, my hand coming to rest over my heart, a demonstration of sincerity.

Halting the patrol via the radio allows us to get chatting in

the middle of the bazaar. In a baker's stall two men are surrounded by rows of fresh naan bread. The younger man is
busy at the oven, while the elder with a white beard is at the
front, selling it.

'Why are you here?' asks the old man.

'To help secure the town so that it can be improved,' I
reply, drawing closer.

'How? What improvements?'

'Well, that's for the people to decide and then the government can make it happen.'

Suddenly I'm aware of how grandiose and pompous I
sound. I can't give concrete examples of 'reconstruction' projects because there aren't any happening – not yet at least. I
want to be able to tell him that there'll be a new school for his
children, electricity, new wells, new roads, but I can't. I now
feel a bit silly. The old man gives a non-committal slow nod
of the head and tugs at his beard. He offers me a naan bread.
I accept and, determined to pay for it, tease out a roll of
Afghanis stuck into the top of my body armour and give him
a fifty note, about a dollar. I fold the crisp bread in half and
stuff it into my map pocket, closing the zip to conceal it. I get
thirty-eight Afghanis back in change, and continue strolling,
with Tamim by my side.

On the other side of the bazaar some of the British soldiers are trying in vain to buy toothbrushes, making up for
the fact that they were 'crashed out' of Camp Bastion with
only their patrolling kit and no personal comforts. With
Tamim's interjection the shopkeeper is very willing to do a
bulk deal: ten brushes for two dollars. The soldiers are
delighted; they can share them out and not have to double

up. Moving to a fruit stall I buy a kilo of mangoes. The young turbaned seller is friendly but uncommunicative. Having paid a couple of ragged Afghani notes, I give the blue plastic bag to Tamim so that I can carry my rifle with both hands.

It's a prosperous place, judging by the array of goods on sale, and cars in a reasonable state of repair pass by frequently. Having come through the main bazaar, we break west and start heading towards the District Centre. As I pass a public call office sign it strikes me as extraordinary that a phone line has reached Sangin. There's also mobile coverage; the Chief is frequently on his cell phone.

Back at the District Centre, I throw my kit into the front of the Snatch and go up onto the roof, just with my rifle and pistol. In the dusk the Chief chatters away with a few of his gang, sitting on plastic garden furniture, having enjoyed the sunset. The slight breeze evaporates the sweat from my shirt and is pleasantly cooling. The Chief looks profoundly calm. His right hand clicks a loop of turquoise prayer beads, his thumb pulling two at a time over the forefinger into his palm. He wears a simple white *shalwar qamiz* and black shoes; they're of a 1970s loafer pattern, black leather with big heels, worn without socks. They're a testament to his status; he can afford not to wear sandals.

Looking north from the roof top I see a series of low bare hills unfolding like a rumpled silk sheet. The Helmand River, broad and fast-flowing, emerges from between them, cradled in broad grey gravel banks, passing the compound not more than a couple of hundred metres distant to the west. Another few hundred metres in the same direction the far side of the Sangin valley rises, barren and abrupt, silhouetted now by a faint bronze glow. To the east, the town sprawls out for a couple of kilometres. Far above the bazaar, a pair of kites engage in a playful staccato dance.

Haji Mirwais, the Chief's second-in-command, offers me his pouch of naswar. Now practised in its use, I accept and place a pinch under my tongue. Reclining in my chair, a tingling relaxation rises, weighing my body down. My thoughts rise in a swirl of ineloquent euphoria. I'm touched by his simple sharing gesture; I feel included.

The Chief stands abruptly and we follow him down the stairs from the roof into his *hijra*. Thin mattresses clad in dark velvet have been placed around the wall. The chief sits opposite the door and I settle on his right as befits my status as his guest. After we begin to chat, however, I place Tamim in between us so he can more easily interpret some of the more difficult and fast-flowing Pashtu. Haji Mirwais is on my right and the rest of the gathering is made up of the Chief's militiamen.

On top of a long orange cloth before us the tea boy places long naan breads, a large metal dish of stew, a plateful of boiled mutton cuts and a plastic basin of whey with a ladle sticking out. I'm the only one given a glass. The Chief fills it and then drinks a long draught directly from the ladle before returning it to the basin, from where it's picked up by another diner. The naan is cold but still fresh and the stew, which turns out to be naan slices drenched in tomato sauce and mutton dripping, is hot and delicious. We use little strips of nan bread as pincer-spoons, deftly arched between the fingers and thumb of the right hand. The chief puts chunks of the choicest mutton – stringy grey meat and bulbous lumps of white fat – onto my piece of bread. Determined to be an ideal guest, I swallow the fat, though it turns my stomach.

When we've eaten our fill, the dishes are removed. All the leftover bread is placed in the middle of the cloth and gathered up into a bundle, ready for the next meal. Tea is served in little glasses and we begin to chat. The Chief is curious about my faith.

'How frequently, Captain, do you pray?'

'Well ... We pray whenever we like, probably once or twice a day.'

'And do you fast?'

'Not really. We can give up something we like for forty days, like chocolate.'

'So, what do *you* give up?'

'Umm ... I gave up grapes last year, and this year I didn't really give up anything.'

The Chief nods and strokes his moustaches, looking slightly nonplussed. His name, Haji Khan Mohammad, reflects the fact that he has completed the Haj, the pilgrimage to Islam's holiest shrine in Mecca, and is clearly devout. My representation of Christian practice seems flimsy and inconsequential, in stark contrast to the faith of the men around me, whose religious fidelity and sense of complete certainty for a brief moment I envy.

Thanking the Chief for supper, I leave the *hijra*, walking out into the warm evening. Our Snatch is parked at the front of the building, backing onto the dirty veranda behind its high stone pillars. Relieving Lance Corporal Bow, I settle down to 'stag on'. He cheerfully extracts his sleeping bag from his kit and leaves for the doss-room opposite the *hijra*. We're sharing it with the ANA, although Captain Ahmed has taken his guys onto the roof to sleep; it's cooler and the wind from the river keeps the mosquitoes away. I sit in the back of the Snatch with the radio set on the vehicle's roof, to get a better signal back to FOB Robinson. Lance Corporal Bow has strung up a tactical radio so we can speak to the British platoon next door. I send a situation report to FOB Robinson telling them that all is well, the platoon house is up and running, and we've had a pretty positive response in the bazaar. In reply I'm told to expect the British Colonel early tomorrow for the Shura.

The night is quiet. I mull over the baker's question from earlier on. It gets me thinking about what the plan for Sangin is exactly. I would like to have given my questioner some better answers about how our presence might improve things. Currently, of the three lines of operation (security, development and governance) much discussed prior to deployment, only the first is present in Sangin. We can provide security by patrolling around the town but we can't start development projects, which are the key to winning hearts and minds. Nor can we get involved in governance and counter-narcotics.

Now that the Army is in Sangin the other agencies should be with us. We've had a friendly response from the population so far and *now* is the time to show them how their livelihoods might be improved by supporting us. This is our window of opportunity. I cast my mind back to the glib jargon I heard from the DfID girl in Colchester before deploying. She needs to be here now with us, making it happen. Initially some 'quick-impact projects' would be ideal – perhaps repaving a road – to generate extra civilian employment and keep the population sweet. A few thousand dollars from their huge budget would be incredibly well spent buying a bit of sympathy from the population until their trust can be won with more enduring projects. Also, the Foreign Office needs to be here providing some public information, telling the population what's going to happen with the poppy, otherwise they'll assume the worst – that we're here simply to put an end to the poppy and destroy their livelihoods.

CHAPTER 8

'As far as I can tell, they're on our side'

May 2006: Sangin, Helmand Province, Afghanistan

Under the mulberry tree the Shura gathers. High green boughs shade white-turbaned elders. The rich mahogany of their faces is amplified by the cleanness of their clothing. Some, with long white beards, are ancient, their bark-like skin deep-lined and wizened. They're unarmed and one old whitebeard has a child cradled on his knee. It's a tender and incongruous sight in a place where a man's hands are normally clutching an AK.

Cross-legged and crammed together on top of a colourful expanse of woven plastic matting, they form an untidy hollow square around Colonel Shirdil, who sits at the base of the tree. Above him a yellow songbird sits in a little cage hanging from a lower bough. The British Colonel and I are on his left.

Shirdil begins: 'In the name of God, the most merciful and beneficent . . . I am from Badakhshan, my father was Tajik but my mother was a Pashtun.'

This means that he understands the Pashtun honour code – the *Pashtunwali* – and wants to help solve their problems. After repeating this sentiment at length he eventually gets around to asking the forty or so elders to voice their concerns. The Chief of Police has been deliberately kept away to allow an honest discussion, and the District Chief has stayed away to keep the whole thing impartial. From the front row of cross-legged figures an old man rises and having, like Shirdil, evoked the name of God with a 'Bismillah ar-rahman ar-rahim', replies:

'The police have beaten many people in this town. They have also taken money from them. There is nothing we can do to stop them . . .'

He continues to give a general description of barbaric police behaviour but does not give any details of specific incidents. Several others do the same. It's clear they're not willing to speak freely, possibly due to the presence of some militia who have slowly gathered at the flanks of the meeting to eavesdrop. This is frustrating; the Shura is supposed to be our chance to get an honest description of the situation in Sangin without local politics interfering. It's impossible to tell who's sent the militia; they may be the District Chief's men or might even have been sent by the Chief of Police. Sensing this, Shirdil gets up and shoos them away. Then he settles back down, and asks the elders to resume their contributions.

An old man stands and, lifting the tail of his shalwar qamiz, reveals some violet bruises just below his rib cage. 'I was beaten by the police after an argument. They wanted money from me . . . What was I to do? I cannot fight them, I am too old.'

He sits back down. No one else seems very keen to offer up any more details so, after a slight pause, the British Colonel describes the proposed solution: a new auxiliary police force nominated by the elders themselves.

'If you choose twenty-four men whom you can trust, they would be the basis of a new police force that is not corrupt and has the support of the people.'

'But these men will have their own loyalties. Each side will plant their own man to spy on the others,' says one old man.

'It's impossible for it not to be corrupted,' adds another.

A succession of negative voices condemn the idea. The rivalries at play in Sangin are clearly more numerous and complex than it might seem to us on the surface. We've very little understanding of a situation probably involving violent blood feuds between tribes and families, narco-economics and Islamic fundamentalism. What knowledge we've gained in the past few days is superficial to say the least and no foundation for making decisions about what to do here now we're in the middle of town. Shirdil invites the elders to come to FOB Robinson the following day to discuss the idea further in private. There's lukewarm acceptance of the invitation and suddenly the sitting mass rises to a stand, breaking into a noisy cacophony of vigorous chatting. The Shura is over. An old man gives Shirdil a handful of fresh purple figs carried in the knotted corner of his shawl. Above him the songbird flutters with agitation at the sudden movement around its cage then comes to an uneasy rest.

The Taliban have not been mentioned at all during the Shura, but the Colonel, standing listening to an old man, suddenly grabs me.

'This old boy says there's Taliban in the bazaar right now. Let's get in there and show 'em who's boss.'

'OK, sir, we'll be there in five minutes,' I reply, making for the Snatch to get the team together.

Ten minutes later we're patrolling into the bazaar. I'm calm but super-alert. I'm at the front with Captain Ahmed and the ANA, followed by two British sections. I've got Finny and Lance Corporal Bow just behind me.

'Keep fucking switched on guys, it might get noisy,' I advise as we turn into the main bazaar.

'Livin' the dream, sir,' replies Private Finau, with only a little bit of irony.

The bazaar is free of Taliban, or at least no one shoots at us. We receive the same discreet friendliness and occasional curiosity as the day before, although it's quiet as no one does their shopping in the midday sun. On the way back in, the British Colonel zooms past in his wagon and gives a wave, on his way back to the FOB. I stop at the fruit stall and buy two small green melons, a gift for the Chief.

Tramping back to the district centre, the sweat streams down my face and back. We should really have had something better to say to the Shura about what we're doing here. The elders have a great deal of influence over the rest of the population, so we if we had a 'reconstruction' line of operation or a poppy alternative we could have been promoting them, rather than just suggesting the half-baked auxiliary police idea which went down like a lead balloon.

Back at the District Centre, I go into the middle room with Shirdil to meet the Security Chief of Sangin. It seems he's another government representative. How his role relates to the District Chief and Police Chief is unclear. We sit on the floor of the dark, dank room. The Security Chief is a big man in his forties with powerful limbs and swollen feet. Dark rings about his eyes and a bulging white turban enhance a look of controlled ferocity.

He leans forward and speaks quickly. 'I am the youngest of three brothers; the eldest is now in the parliament in Kabul, my other brother was murdered by the Taliban. That is why I want to kill them.'

Colonel Shirdil takes notes; these become a list of suspected Taliban and their locations, mainly villages in the north of the valley. The Security Chief is adamant that the details should be noted correctly and uses his hands a lot, drawing illustrations on the palm of his left with the forefinger of his right. He has lots to say and Shirdil's list grows. Tamim is also taking notes in my pocket book, scribbling quickly with a blue ballpoint; the lilting Persian script is beautiful though hastily formed. The Security Chief does not accuse the District Chief of any Taliban involvement but the fact that he's not in the room with us and we're here without his knowledge suggests to me that, oddly, he is not trusted. Having said his piece, the Security Chief trails into silence. He's assured by Shirdil that the information will be acted upon and sent up to the British and Afghan headquarters. As we shake hands and leave the murky room I reckon that, given our intelligence vacuum in Sangin right now, this information could be priceless.

Now at 1500 the afternoon heat is overwhelming. It pounds down like an invisible suffocating blanket. Lance Corporal Bow is stagging on in the back of the Snatch, picking at a ration pack.

'How's it going, Corporal B?' I ask.

'Yeah, all right, boss,' he replies in his cheerful Essex lilt. 'I was gonna eat but my guts feel a bit weird.'

'Go and sleep, I'll stag on.'

'Nah, you're all right, boss, Finny's taking over in a minute anyway.'

Cheered by his good humour, I go myself to our doss-room. Manipulating my body armour into a reluctant pillow, I stretch out on the stained carpet with my rifle tucked in beside me. Despite the fetid stench of new sweat and ancient dirt I succumb immediately to the afternoon's soporific power.

Two hours later I'm on the roof with the Disctrict Chief's second-in-command, Haji Mirwais. We're due to patrol out shortly so I'm scanning around the town with my binoculars just in case anything of interest is happening.

Haji Mirwais clearly knows about the meeting with the Security Chief. 'Maybe Captain, he gave you names of the Taliban in Sangin?'

'Mmm . . . Maybe. I wasn't really listening.'

'Many people that he says are Taliban are the ones he does not like, the ones he has a feud against,' he says quietly. 'He wants you to help him.'

'It's a very complicated situation, I think,' I say, in complete honesty

'Captain, in your home do you have a girlfriend?' he asks with a smile

'Yes, I do,' I reply, amused by the very abrupt change of subject

'So, you are enjoying lubshub?' he asks with a raised brow

'Lubshub?' Turning to Tamim, I find him chuckling gently.

Happily he interprets: 'Yes, loveshove, you know, when you are together with your girlfriend,' he explains, rubbing his pointed index fingers back and forth, side by side, in demonstration

'Oh, right, *loveshove* – yes, of course! I enjoy it whenever possible.'

Laughing at the sudden appearance of this rhyming slang, which Tamim later explains is a Hindi film import, the thought of gorgeous Lucy in idyllic Oxfordshire seems almost too remote to even believe. Like many others, I have stripped my kit of all pictures and addresses of loved ones. Intended as a security measure, it also prevents distracting memories of whoever you're missing. Her face floods into my mind and then vanishes as I clamber down from the roof to get my patrol kit ready.

Leaving the District Centre on foot, we patrol northwards following a deep, fast-flowing irrigation channel which runs parallel to the river and passes the District Centre at the foot of its compound. To our right, small fields of rich green wheat are tightly interwoven with mud-built farmsteads and great clumps of mulberry trees. Drenched in the orange light of early evening, the wheat stalks are buffeted slightly by the pleasant breeze coming off the river. Leaving the mud track we break east into the farmland, stepping carefully along an intricate network of irrigation streams. Javed is on point about ten metres ahead of me, with Captain Ahmed just behind him looking back every few paces for my directions.

The farmland surrounding us is incredibly fertile, well nurtured and orderly. There appears to be little if any poppy grown in this ultra-fertile zone; wheat is probably the priority near the water as it's a very thirsty crop. Without stopping, I pick sweet white mulberries as I pass under their heavily laden boughs and stuff them into my mouth.

Approaching a farmstead, Tamim, off to my left, raises his hand suddenly. 'Stop! stop! There is a girl washing,' he says, retreating and pointing over his shoulder. A blue shawl briefly flickers behind a row of trees.

'Hey Javed! Ahmed Jaan! Let's go!' I shout, waving them back towards me. We backtrack.

Tamim, at my side, is shaken. 'If we go near their women, they will kill us.'

Giving the dwelling a wide berth, we continue on our route. Keeping a sharp lookout for people, I hope that the blue shawl, the first glimpse I've had of a woman in Sangin, is also my last.

We're in a difficult position in Sangin; we need to 'dominate' the town with patrols to show its inhabitants that we're securing it, but this in itself might cause offence. Just the presence of a bunch of British soldiers – even with a few Afghans mixed in – is potentially deeply antagonistic, especially if the majority of the population aren't aware of our purpose. This is a tribal society that adheres strictly to a code of honour, the *Pashtunwali*, and will not hesitate, as Tamim has pointed out, to respond violently to any offence. We must be careful not to blunder around, otherwise we'll end up becoming a big target for everyone, not just the Taliban.

As the fields are gradually replaced by scruffy concrete compounds we come to the main road, the 611. We're north of the bazaar at this point and, crossing the road, we head past a vast cemetery that dominates the eastern half of the town centre. The dusty, barren expanse is covered with grave mounds, their ends adorned with pairs of fragmented flat stones poking up in opposite diagonals. Some graves are further marked by large green flags, the colour of Islamic obeisance. A stone pillar and a clutch of green and black flags mark a shrine of some sort. Keen to avoid it, we move quickly past it away from the cemetery.

Having crossed the 611 again, we head through more close-knit agricultural dwellings and fields, back towards the District Centre. I'm pleased that we've been literally right around Sangin, unhindered. We have, it seems, complete freedom of movement.

Back at the District Centre I stag on in the back of the Snatch. I give a 'sitrep' – a situation report – to the headquarters in FOB Robinson, telling them what we've been doing, and then set about cleaning my rifle.

Sangin is really quite prosperous, judging by the rich farmland, the well-stocked bazaar and the numerous cars on the main road. The economy seems to be booming, and of course this is on the back of the poppy grown throughout the region. Sangin, I'm guessing, is the centre of the opium trade for the north of Helmand, where opium barons, having collected the harvest from local cash-croppers, sell on the unrefined opium to traffickers who'll take it either north through the Hindu Kush and onwards to Central Asia or south to Pakistan.

There's clearly a thriving, lucrative industry in Sangin which will make it a really tough nut to crack: what we offer as an alternative to the poppy will have to be equally lucrative, or perhaps made more attractive by additional developmental benefits like healthcare and education. I'm now slightly desperate to know what the alternative will be and hoping that the development people and the Foreign Office are going to put in an appearance soon.

Near the back of the wagon a few of the Chief's militia are leaning around a motorcycle that is a faithful replica of a Japanese original, only the name badge is imperfect – it's upside down and reads HODNA.

Intrigued by my presence, one of the militiamen wanders over and leans on the back door. Not much more than a gangly youth, his beard is short and wispy. A thick thatch of black hair emerges in a messy fringe from the arched front of his shiny prayer cap, adorned with plastic gems.

He peers quizzically in. 'What are you doing?'

'Listening,' I reply, pointing to the headset on my left ear.

Nodding, he takes a small comb from the chest pocket of his grimy brown *shalwar qamiz* and runs it through his beard. An AK is slung comfortably under his arm, decorated with tight bindings of pink plastic cable and little reflective stickers of holy Qur'anic calligraphy. A pink nylon flower pokes from its muzzle. He strikes me as rather whimsical, hardly the fearsome Mujahid of Afghan legend. One of his fellow militiamen appears by his side and stares at me. His bloodshot eyes, lined with black kohl, are watery and blinking. I ask for the comb, and it's handed to me. I run it through my beard, pleased that my growth far exceeds theirs. I'm fond of my beard; it's like a calendar of my time with the Afghan Army, a physical testament to being 'out there', immersed in a foreign culture. I draw the comb from my ears down to my chin, enjoying its cleansing, scratchy relief. I then bush out the sides, adding as much volume as possible.

As I hand the comb back, the militiaman refuses it. 'Keep it, it's spoilt now.'

His words sting me. 'Very well,' I reply. 'I'll treat it as a gift.'

But it is not. He has made plain his contempt for me as an unclean infidel. It's disheartening: I regard my beard as a cultural asset, a symbol of maturity and social standing; but it now seems a bit superficial. I put the comb in my pocket as the militiamen wander off.

Having been relieved by Finny, I go up to the roof to sleep. The night's breeze is preferable to the stench and stuffiness of the doss-room, which now reeks of sweaty feet and old food; the tea-boy has left a pot of stew in there to store overnight. The rooftop is scattered with prostrate sleepers. In a corner a pair of militiamen are on sentry behind a barricade of leaking sandbags. They sit on white plastic chairs and survey the river. Unrolling a blanket, I can see the top of the Snatch wagon just below me. Over by the main gate a gaggle of militia sit in a circle under the birdcage, talking quietly and smoking hashish; a peal of helpless laughter occasionally rings out. Lying on top of the blanket I cover myself with my sleeping bag and, enjoying the brilliant stars, drift off.

Back on stag in the small hours I sit uncomfortably in the wagon. Before dawn the militia descend from the roof for prayers. Immediately adjacent to the District Centre a small mud building serves as a mosque, recognisable as such only by a loudspeaker attached to a crooked wooden pole at its front. It has a pretty little pale blue door and window. The men make their ablutions in a fast-flowing irrigation stream next to the mosque. The loudspeaker seems not to work and they make their way silently to prayer.

We're due out on patrol at five, so just beforehand Lance Corporal Bow comes and transfers the radio from the top of the wagon into his backpack.

As dawn breaks we're heading south through small farmsteads. As usual I've got the ANA at the front with me. Moving around a field of wheat along a narrow path, we're overtaken on our flank by the British soldiers from the rear of the patrol moving straight through it, leaving trails of trampled stalks.

Moving back along the path, I ask the Lieutenant commanding them to steer his men onto the path. 'Otherwise the farmer will be a bit gutted to find our tracks.'

The Lieutenant's response is suddenly angry. Perhaps upset at being given advice in front of his men, he flares up. 'Mind your own fuckin' business, my blokes know what they're doing. You're just along for the ride,' he spits out.

'What? If it weren't for the ANA we wouldn't be on this patrol, *they* make it possible, we've got to do everything with them – that's the whole fucking point,' I retort.

An awkward silence settles and I turn away, moving back along the path. By now the tail end of the patrol is moving through the field so I jog along the path to get back to the front. Rather than angered, I'm disappointed by the platoon commander. I know he's tired and under pressure but he should realise it's supposed to be a 'joint' operation with the ANA. Their presence is small but of critical importance, isn't it? Without Javed and Captain Ahmed at the front of the patrol surely we'd appear as a bunch of foreigners doing our own thing. Perhaps we do anyway, despite their presence? Really, the patrol should be all Afghans with a couple of Brits giving advice, but that's not going to happen if our Kandak continues to sit tight in the FOB. As for the wheat, it's not the end of the world but we must try to avoid offending people whenever possible.

Having emerged from the farmland, we move onto the 611 and head north, towards the bazaar. Captain Ahmed stops for a chat with the man running the southern petrol pump. Drawing close, I greet him and accept his offer of a glass of water. He's short and grimy with a straggling grey beard.

Despite his humble appearance he has a keen curiosity. 'Tell me, are you going to prohibit the growing of poppy?' he asks, smiling.

'Well, we will offer an alternative – something else for people to grow ...'

'What?' he asks, still smiling.

'Well, it's not certain, but there will be other benefits, like improvements in the town ... That is, development,' I reply, disappointed at the hollowness of my words.

Sensing my unease, he does not question me further, but makes a prediction. 'If you try to stop the poppy in Sangin, there will be much trouble,' he says, his smile now replaced by a look of mild anguish.

'We won't do anything too hasty, I can assure you,' I reply, sensing that his words are very true.

Thanking him for the glass of water, I bid farewell with my hand on my heart. The gesture is returned. Captain Ahmed and I return to the road and the patrol continues.

Passing through the bazaar, we receive the usual discreet

friendliness and passive stares. I quickly purchase a kilo of small yellow mangoes. From the bazaar we move westwards, down into the dry riverbed, and head back towards the District Centre. The riverbed is full of livestock, at least two hundred head. Brown jostling flocks of sheep and goats are attended by men and boys, some catching animals, some conversing at the side. As I approach, their sun-darkened faces become clearer, adorned with long unkempt beards and simple off-white prayer caps. These men are the Koochi, a nomadic Pashtun tribe of herders. Grazing their beasts across all of south and east Afghanistan, they dwell in tents and visit towns to sell their livestock. They're shocked to see us.

Catching the gaze of two men who appear to have stopped their conversation mid-flow, I greet them. 'Salaam alaykum.'

They stare intently at me, without response.

'When do you hold this market?' I ask, undeterred.

Judging that my presence has stunned them into silence and they're unable to understand my artless Pashtu, I move away to look at the herd while Tamim converses with them. The sheep and goats chew their cud hurriedly. They seem healthy and have bloated, wobbling tails of fat which make them look ridiculous. Leaving them behind, we head towards to the District Centre which is nearby, at the end of the riverbed. Tamim tells me that the livestock market happens twice a week, on Mondays and Thursdays.

Having returned to the compound, I join Captain Ahmed and his men for breakfast. We settle down in a small circle on the plastic matting under the mulberry tree. It's an idyllic setting: the morning sun, yet to gain its ferocity, bathes the garden in a soft light, catching pink cherry blossom and small orange flowers among the grass. It's like a bizarre military picnic. Captain Ahmed offers me the ladle from a basin of whey. I drink and return it. Tearing strips of fresh naan bread, we plunge them into plates of thick clotted cream sprinkled with coarse white sugar. It's utterly delicious. Soon finished, it's followed by little greengages and tea. I mull over my argument with the platoon commander. I'm fond of Ahmed and his little band of men. So far they've been reliable and perfectly willing. Though small in number, they do at least give us a bit of an 'Afghan face' and hopefully more credibility among the population. I'm hoping that one of our ANA companies might soon replace the British platoon so that there only have to be a couple of Brits in the District Centre and it's the ANA running the show.

A Pashtun in his early thirties, Captain Ahmed has crooked dirty teeth and a short beard sprouting in scraggly patches. Soft-spoken and very patient, he seems to be well-liked by his soldiers. He's not really a talker and says the odd word to his men but not much else. I tell him that I'm grateful for his help with the patrolling and that he and his team will probably be relieved tonight by a new team from the FOB. He nods happily.

As his soldiers get up and leave he says quietly, 'Captain Leo, remember that everyone here has some connection to the poppy, even the Chief, everyone . . .'

'Surely the Chief is trying to stop it – no?' I ask, with deliberate naivety.

'He'll do whatever is most beneficial for him in all things. If the Taliban are here he'll support the Taliban, when the British are here he supports the British.'

His words trail off as one of the militia walks behind us to the mulberry tree and takes down the songbird's cage.

I'm unsure how seriously to take Captain Ahmed's warning, but to be honest I don't feel unsafe at the moment. I'm not stupid enough to believe that everyone is on our side and I'm well aware of the duplicitous nature of Afghan politics, but so far I trust the Chief, or at least trust him enough to feel he wouldn't endanger our lives while we're on his turf. What would be the point of that? Like everyone else he's keen to hedge his bets.

Even so, after today's patrol I do feel an increasing uneasiness about the clumsy, ill-informed nature of our presence in Sangin. We're running the risk of offending people simply by being here, but we're not using the opportunity to achieve anything. Good intentions and hand-shaking will count for nothing without anything concrete to back them up. We desperately need some proper intelligence people from Helmand Task Force headquarters to help us work out what's going on in Sangin with local politics, opium and the Taliban, and the bureaucrats from DfID and the FCO need to get up here and get busy alongside us.

After thanking Captain Ahmed for breakfast, I go through the garden down to the irrigation channel, following the man with the birdcage. The channel is a dozen feet wide, with deep, fast-flowing blue-green water. On the bank, shaded by dense greenery, the man is squatting on his haunches, washing the cage, splashing handfuls of water across its floor. The songbird rests unsteadily at the top of the cage, surrounded by pink plastic flowers. The man refills a little water vessel attached to the bars of the cage. From a bag in his pocket he pours a small amount of birdseed into a tiny dish, and places it carefully inside. Seeing that he's happily absorbed in his task, I leave him and wander back up towards the District Centre.

On the radio in the back of the wagon, I speak to HQ. We've still not received any orders about how long we're here for and who else might be joining us but I'm hoping to get clarification of this from whoever brings our water and rations resupply. I'm told that it'll come some time today. Tamim and Finny are waiting at the back of the wagon, listening in; they break out into big smiles when they hear about the resupply as they're both due to go on R&R, and they need to get back to the FOB to catch the Chinook when it flies in tomorrow.

As I slump in the back of the wagon, listless with the rising heat, a Toyota Land Cruiser screeches to a halt and disgorges a group of the District Chief's men. From the back they unload what looks like a pair of black footballs swaddled in thick white polythene, and bustle excitedly into the *hijra*.

'What's that?' I ask Haji Mirwais as he follows them in.

'It is opium, it's been confiscated and will be destroyed.' Without stopping he disappears into the *hijra*, firmly closing the door.

Incredulous, my confidence in the Chief and his men is shaken. As Captain Ahmed warned, *everyone* is connected to the poppy in some way. I want to believe that it really will be destroyed but I just can't be sure.

The resupply arrives in the early evening and brings rations and water but no new information about who's coming to join us or the plan as a whole for Sangin. As we unload boxes of MREs and mineral water, one of the sergeants with the resupply looks wide-eyed at a gaggle of militia gathered by the front gate.

'Fucking 'ell, sir, d'you feel safe here?'

'Yeah, we're all right, we've got mangoes and everything,' I reply, keen to jest.

'What about this lot? They look a bit nuts to me,' he says, glancing again at the militia, now sitting in an untidy circle, generating thick plumes of smoke.

'They're OK. As far as I can tell, they're on our side,' I say, half-convincingly.

With the resupply, Captain Ahmed and his guys are replaced with a new team of ANA, four young Tajiks. It seems that no more ANA are available.

As the resupply convoy leaves, I'm fairly gutted that no one has arrived to give our presence here more purpose and nothing seems to have been developed in terms of the plan for Sangin as a whole. I feel like we're sitting here wasting precious time while the Helmand Task Force headquarters appear to be doing nothing about it. I'm not sure that things will be peaceful for much longer; we're a fairly big target and the Taliban, or whoever, are most probably sizing us up before making their move. Unless we show the population some sort of progress they won't support us when the shooting starts and may even turn against us.

'Where the fuck is the DfID bird now?' I ask myself, irate with disappointment.

If they're too risk-averse to come into Sangin then we ought really have a bag of money ourselves to start some high-profile basic projects, to buy some sympathy until the real development can start. 'Whatever the Comprehensive Approach was supposed to be,' I tell myself, 'this is not it!'

Declining supper with the Chief, I bed down in the doss-room with a churning in my guts. Shortly I'm gripped with stomach cramps and, grabbing my head-torch, scurry through the dark garden to the stinking squat toilet and submit to a paroxysm of uncontrollable liquid-shit diarrhoea. Standing up, I move out of the toilet, pausing next to a patch of six-foot sunflowers. My stomach turns as my mouth is filled with a rush of water. Heaving, I vomit great arcs of toxic yellow puke, exploding through my throat and splashing onto the sunflower stalks. With eyes watering I shudder between each round, desperate not to taste the remnants stuck at the back of my mouth.

After the convulsions have subsided I return gingerly to the doss-room. I'm passed by Lance Corporal Bow heading for where I've just been, with the same affliction. It seems that while sleeping in the doss-room, the filth has penetrated our bodies. Curling up on the greasy carpet, clutching my stomach, every fibre of my body screams 'sickness'. I'm exhausted and yet I cannot sleep.

CHAPTER 9

'It seems we've been played'

May 2006: Sangin, Helmand Province, Afghanistan

Wrenched from a half-slumber by a hand on my shoulder, I make my way to the Snatch wagon to stag on. In the grey light of early dawn, I relieve the new driver who replaced Finny yesterday. Light-headed and dry-mouthed, I break open a bottle of mineral water and down it steadily. Up until now I've been drinking the local water from a tank in the doss-room which has chunks of ice floating in it. The militiamen bring in a great block of ice daily, and it sits slowly melting on the floor of the dusty veranda as they hack bits off whenever they feel like it. An ice-cold drink of water here is simply luxurious; however, I reckon I ought to stick to mineral water until I'm better. The quivering in my bowels has subsided a little and although I'm chronically dehydrated from all the puking, that's now passed, probably because I've nothing left to puke up. I reckon if I fast for the day and just drink water I'll be back to normal by tonight.

Lance Corporal Bow, however, has got more puking to do and has visited the toilet three times in the last hour.

'Fucking hell, Corporal B, you may as well just stay down there!' I call out after him as he scurries past again.

'I need the exercise, boss.'

Moments later great strangled heaves sound from the toilet as he retches repeatedly, with impressive vigour.

By the afternoon, Lance Corporal Bow is still puking, and although I'm feeling a bit better, I've still got the shits. I'm now keen for him to see a doctor.

On the radio my request for our team to be rotated with another is agreed in the late afternoon. After rapidly bidding farewell to the Chief, assuring him we'll be replaced and thanking him for his hospitality, we leave the District Centre, waving the militiamen goodbye. Numbed by the illness, I'm ambivalent about leaving. Anyway, I expect I'll be back in a few days.

Back at FOB Robinson we find the mentoring team having a barbecue. They've rigged up half an oil drum, now full of embers, and a griddle of American-issue burgers and spare ribs. They're from ten-man ration packs and come with burger buns sealed in green foil vacuum packs which taste like cream crackers dipped in paraffin. I nibble the corner of a spare rib and decide to continue my fast for a bit longer.

Colonel Shirdil is there, munching a burger, and I can't help thinking he should be getting a grip of his Kandak and getting some troops together to replace the British platoon at the District Centre. Moving to one side of the barbecue, I back-brief the commander of the British team that's about to go down there, telling him what the situation is and where exactly we've been on patrol.

After unloading my kit from the Snatch I tramp through the ankle-deep dust to our corner of the compound. A new construction has emerged: up against the wall next to the camouflage net three plywood walls sprouting four-inch nails are covered by a battered tarpaulin to form a room.

CSM Johnstone appears from a tarpaulin flap at the side. 'Fuckin' hell, sir, I thought you'd gone native. Welcome back.'

'Thanks! I can see you've been busy,' I reply, ducking through the door flap

'Just tryin' tae get us some shelter frae this bastard dust.'

Inside, a waxy yellow light and stifling heat are generated by the afternoon sun. The CSM has set up our mosquito nets on sheets of plywood and arranged old ammunition tins as seats, so it's looking pretty homely. It's just me and him in here; Finny got away on the Chinook for R&R and Stoddy is bunking up with the American medic in the American training team's compound. Apparently we're due to move over there when the Americans leave with the Herati Kandak. Until then we're making do, but the new shelter looks fairly pukka.

Outside I look under my poncho: the wind has brought an inch of dust into my former wardrobe. Toppling it over, I move it into our new home. Laid sideways, it provides an excellent tabletop. Hanging my kit on an array of four-inch nails I feel content with my new bed space. Taking my pistol I move back outside, wandering over to the plunge pool.

When the American Special Forces first constructed the camp, the land was leased from a local farmer on the condition that the Americans enabled him to continue to draw water from a well on the site. Their engineer, clearly a bright spark, created a system of pipes with a pump to channel water through the perimeter and sensibly included a deep plunge pool in the system, made from a plastic water tank cut in half. Happily, the troops inside the perimeter get to wash properly and the farmer's crop, which naturally is poppy, flourishes.

Keeping my combats on I jump into the pool, four feet square, and submerge myself fully in the wonderfully cool, cleansing water. Sitting briefly on the bottom, I blow a flurry of bubbles through the water. Standing, I scrub my beard and head with soap and, taking off my combats, scrub them too. Wearing only my dog-tags, I lather up and submerge, over and over. I feel invigorated and well again. The illness and filth of the District Centre have been washed away. I put my boots and wet combats back on and stroll towards our shack, drying as I walk in the evening sun.

I'm not clean for very long. CSM Johnstone and I weigh down the door flap with ammunition boxes under the strange blue light of a cylume, a chemical light stick which once initiated glows for a couple of hours. The door flap however, part of an old tent, is an imperfect fit and can't stop the dust billowing in defiantly after each gust of wind.

I'm resigned and the CSM is angry. 'I'm fuckin' threaders wi' this. It's the worst place I've ever been.'

But despite his venom I know that he's simultaneously relishing the challenge, the feeling of being 'out there' in this almost comically absurd filthy hole.

By the time I crawl into my mosquito net I'm ingrained with dust. A thick uniform layer has settled on my sleeping bag. I stretch out, masking my face with a cotton sweat rag. I'm woken from a stifled sleep by the battering of the wind on our fragile walls. The cylume has dimmed and though I can't see the dust that penetrates our walls I can feel it accumulating about my head.

In the morning, the wind has gone. I break my fast with pineapples in syrup from an American ration pack and make my way down to the ANA side of the base to find HQ Company. They're located in a watchtower on the west side of the perimeter, overlooking the river and the 611 road.

Ramadan the tea boy is cooking and greets me with a smile. 'Salaam alaykum. How are you, Captain?'

'Alaykum salaam. I'm very well, Ramadan. Where is Captain Hameed?'

'In the river, washing,' he replies, pointing down the dusty slope in front of us towards the green foliage of the river bank. In among the trees a couple of ANA vehicles are parked up and some figures are splashing around in the shallows.

The watchtower, a tall construction of sandbags and timber, is well ordered with clean plastic floor matting. It's homely because they live in it. On the high, narrow windows, facing all directions, rests an array of Kalashnikov weapons including a long sniper rifle. Pir Ahmed arrives and we drink tea sitting outside, facing the river. The company seems to be a bit thin on the ground, and they can't all be in the river.

'Pir Ahmed, where are all your men?'

'On leave, Captain. We have only eighteen men in the company now, so we can only just man our two watchtowers.'

This is sickening. With so few men HQ Company is hamstrung and ineffectual, just like the Kandak as a whole. At this rate the battalion will never be able to find sufficient men to increase the ANA presence at the District Centre in Sangin, especially as Colonel Shirdil isn't keen on the idea anyway. The company's inability to actually do anything due to a lack of manpower has been a persistent theme since the first day of training and I'm now utterly frustrated by it.

Sighing with resignation I move on to a practical issue that we hopefully *can* solve. 'Pir Ahmed, could you by any chance find me a kettle?'

Without speaking he jumps up, has a quick rummage inside the watchtower, and reappears with a shiny tin kettle, its new golden glaze untarnished. 'Take it, Captain, it's yours.'

Having dug a shallow pit next to our shack, I get a little fire going with some timber fragments, leftovers from CSM Johnstone's building frenzy. I rest the kettle over the flames on a trio of stones; its 'Made in China' sticker quickly ignites as the kettle blackens. I'm chuffed at Pir Ahmed's kind gift; not only is it better than an issue mess tin for brewing up in, but we can also heat our MRE packets in it rather than using the fiddly chemical-reaction heaters that come with each pack and never really get them piping hot.

Seeking some more substantial fuel I make for the large pile of firewood outside the baker's hut and notice that the door is ajar and nobody is there. Inside, the deep pit of the oven is cold and a few plastic vessels and rags are all that remain on the dusty floor. Mohammad Qasim has gone, probably back to Gereshk. Deflated, I gather an armful of wood and continue brewing up.

After tea I make my way over to our makeshift headquarters, as I'm the 'watchkeeper' – the officer on duty overnight. On the way I pass the British 105mm gun line, a messy concoction of shelters gathered under a suspended parachute to the rear of the big guns. At the side, a group of young British Artillery soldiers, tattooed, deep brown and dusty, take turns on a pull-up bar. Wearing shorts made from cut-off combat trousers and boots, their shouts of encouragement mingle with cries of mock-derision and laughter.

The operations room is in a watchtower on top of the mud building that houses the American training team. Climbing up the rickety wooden steps onto the flat roof, I remember meeting the Alabama National Guard guys up here and being surprised at their .38 hunting rifle, but it doesn't seem so bizarre now. This is where all operations are supposedly controlled from. Crucially, it's the communications hub of the unit. As the overnight watchkeeper I must be ready to react to any event that might occur involving our troops on the ground and get the more senior officers like the Colonel out of bed if anything really serious occurs. It's basically the same as stagging on except you've got a couple of signallers with you, listening to the radios.

Settling down on a piece of battered garden furniture, I scan the horizon with binoculars. The sun is now a fat glowing orange, falling rapidly towards the horizon. The river reflects its light and is, quite simply, beautiful. I can see the grey mass of the town but no real details. The two signallers with me have a radio each; one's listening to the Helmand Task Force channel, the other to our team at the District Centre. I'm hoping for a quiet night so I can doze in my chair; the best thing about being up here tonight is that I'm away from the evil dust.

At around midnight the team commander at the District Centre comes on the radio and says he's received a warning from the District Chief. Apparently there's a Taliban convoy heading for the District Centre, intending to attack it. This is serious. I inform Helmand Task Force headquarters, and the Colonel's second-in-command, a Major, rushes up to speak to the District Centre on the radio.

The team commander's voice is terse. 'We've got a Taliban convoy approaching from the north . . . probably four vehicles . . . I request aviation to take a look and HE [high explosive] and illum [illumination] on standby . . .'

'Roger . . . Wait,' replies the Major. Grabbing the other radio, he fires off a series of questions and then resumes his previous conversation. 'We can't get aviation for another forty-five minutes but you can have illum.'

Minutes later there's a series of almighty poundings from the gun line. A white spark ignites in the black sky, at least six kilometres away. Its brilliance increases as it floats slowly downwards and then splutters out, just as the next one has reached its climax – the six rounds are perfectly timed to give a continuous screen of light.

However, the commander is unsure what he's seeing. 'Mmm . . . There are two vehicles in the riverbed due north . . . They've got their four-way flashers on . . . Request more illum on the same location.'

Another six rounds are fired up.

'They're leaving . . . They're driving off.'

It sounds a bit bizarre. I've not heard of the Taliban driving around with their hazard lights on.

The team commander comes back on the radio. 'I think this is just bullshit to test our reactions . . . The Chief keeps asking when the helicopter's coming . . . I think we're being tested.'

It seems we've been played. I know the Chief is a bit of a shady character but I'm reluctant to believe he's set on betraying us to the Taliban. Perhaps he's testing us for his own reasons or perhaps it's just a muddle and the vehicles really were a Taliban convoy and were scared off by the illumination. The only thing that's certain is that the team in the District Centre are not happy. 'We do *not* feel safe here . . . The militia are threatening us,' says the commander, now agitated. 'I request to extract at first light.'

'OK, if you don't feel safe then extract,' replies the second-in-command, deflated.

I'm also disappointed, or rather, confused. We simply don't know who's for us and who's against us, yet without any intelligence sources we're unable to find out. Either way the town's inhabitants must have been entertained by the fireworks: they were probably glad it wasn't high-explosive shells we were chucking into town. By the time I come off stag the team has extracted from the District Centre, so there's no one at all in Sangin. Perhaps it's a good thing, seeing as nothing is happening with the reconstruction side of the operation, and they won't just be sitting there like a big target waiting to be hit.

Plodding back through the fine ankle-deep dust towards our shack, I pass the gun line again. They're taking advantage of the cool of the early morning to clean one of their guns, thrusting a great cleaning rod down the long barrel like a Napoleonic naval gun crew. Chattering away, their banter is boisterous; they're clearly jubilant that, after two weeks of tedium in the filthy dust, they've finally fired their guns.

Back in the shack, I get a brew on with CSM Johnstone. He was put on standby to go out with the Quick Reaction Force.

This group would have gone to support our team at the District Centre if it had 'gone noisy' when the illum went up. Consequently he's been up most of the night.

'I dinnae mind. I'd rather be sat in a wagon waitin' to go than tryin' to sleep in this sandpit.'

Agreeing with his sentiment, I make us instant white tea using the sachets of powder. These only come in British ration packs, so I was delighted to be able to liberate them from a box of 'Menu A' that I found while watchkeeping. Two sachets of tea and one of sugar is the perfect combination. I make the CSM's in his issue black half-pint mug and, having lost my issue mug, use the bottom half of a mineral water bottle, which warps slightly as I pour in the boiling water.

Our peace is interrupted by the beating of a Chinook's twin rotor blades. One circles high above us in protective over-watch as its partner, like a massive squat insect, swoops down towards the landing site outside the FOB, generating a sudden dust storm. I clamber onto the perimeter to watch. Static, with its rotors still turning, the helicopter disgorges a gaggle of troops from its tailgate, who make a crouched run off the landing site. Another gaggle makes the opposite movement and, tailgate up, the Chinook promptly rises directly upwards, banks sharply and quickly fades away. Just beyond our perimeter a group of ANA are left among the scattered remnants of their makeshift watchtower, blasted apart by the Chinook's downdraught. Laughing, they half-heartedly set about collecting the pieces.

The troops who've arrived on the Chinook turn out to be a platoon of Gurkhas, to replace the British platoon that's just left on the same helicopter. Having been called to the operations room by the British second-in-command, I meet their platoon commander, an attentive softly-spoken Nepali CSM. I'm required to go with them to recce a location for a new platoon house in Sangin. The Colonel, who's gone to Camp Bastion, has directed that we must get back into town. We're going to the Security Chief's house this time, and I'm required because I've met him.

In the mid-afternoon we rattle into town with the Gurkhas. The Security Chief's house is at the north end of town, beyond the bazaar. It's a vast concrete pile, surrounded by a high-walled compound. Having parked up we have to wait a few minutes for the Security Chief to appear from an outbuilding, as he wasn't expecting us. He has to send one of his lackeys to find the key to the main house. He gives me a smile of recognition as we enter. Although it's empty at the moment the security Chief is not willing to let us use his compound as a base.

'My wife and children will soon be moving in here, for their security. With my wife present I regret that it would be impossible for your troops to be here.'

Despite this, he says at length that he's very keen to help us fight the Taliban and that his men know how to use a GPS. After speaking he takes off his dark turban and re-winds it over his little white skullcap. His deft strokes are a joy to watch. The left hand feeds the material upwards, the right winds it, using the palm then the back of the hand in an unconscious rhythm.

The unlived-in house has a musty smell. It's grand but horribly tacky; the room we're in has a thick fitted carpet, decorative wooden cladding on the walls and a faux-gold door handle. Getting up to leave, we make a cordial farewell.

It's unfortunate that we can't use the Security Chief's compound; it would afford excellent arcs of view over across the northern half of Sangin. I don't really buy his excuse for not having us there, but it's hardly surprising that he doesn't want his fancy new house turned into a patrol base by a gang of foreign soldiers about whom the population may not be ultimately very sympathetic. Though he supports us – from what I've seen so far – it's probably a bit much to ask to have us in his house. Anyway we may as well just mount patrols from the FOB; it's much more discreet than staying in the town.

Driving back into the FOB, I'm surprised to see some new arrivals spread out in the middle of our compound, sorting through their kit. It turns out to be a few EOD (Explosive Ordnance Disposal) bomb-disposal blokes and a UAV (Unmanned Aerial Vehicle) team. They've got a little hand-launched radio-controlled aircraft from which a camera beams back a bird's-eye view of the ground. This is good news; the next time we get a threat warning we can send the UAV up to take a look before putting troops onto the ground. Unfortunately it doesn't work at night but still, it's a step in the right direction. But there are no military intelligence personnel, nor any development or Foreign Office people among the group of dusty new arrivals. Baffled by their absence, I return to the shack.

Stripping off my webbing vest and body armour, I vent my disgust to CSM Johnstone, who is reassuringly sanguine.

'Dinnae worry aboot that lot, sir, they'll be sittin' on their arses wi' fuckin' air-con in Kandahar.'

The following day the Gurkhas deploy to the police station, to use it as new platoon house. Surprised, I discuss it with the second-in-command, who, with the Colonel away in Camp Bastion, is overworked and fed up.

'The Colonel has directed them to occupy the police station so that's where they're going.'

'But surely the Chief of Police is just as bad as the District Chief or probably worse, isn't he?'

'Well, maybe, but we need to be in town . . . and we're not going to find anywhere better,' he says, exhausted.

'But all the civilians hate the Chief of Police, that much we do know.'

'Well, we haven't got any choice really.'

What makes it even more absurd is that no ANA at all are going along. They're supposedly all occupied guarding watchtowers, down to the last man. That means none of the mentoring team will be there either. The police compound really isn't an ideal platoon house; apart from the fact that the Chief of Police is probably a murderous criminal, the town can't be clearly seen from it and it's vulnerably exposed to the hills on its eastern side.

'Christ! This is a pantomime,' I exclaim to myself.

A grim realisation falls over me: there is no plan at all behind any of this. What I had suspected is now suddenly clear. Its not that we're struggling to implement it, it simply doesn't exist. A series of disjointed ill-considered directives from headquarters is all that exists here. Everything else, all the well-meaning reconstruction stuff, is an illusion. The setting up of the platoon house and the time spent there now seem to have been an egotistical folly.

'This is a cluster-fuck,' I gasp under my breath. 'If it wasn't dangerous it would be laughable.'

At this moment the fact that we're surrounded by the hostile sands of the 'Desert of Death' no longer seems funny.

Despairing, I give the Gurkha commander a patrol trace – a sheet of clear plastic on which I've drawn coloured lines marking our routes in town. When he puts it against his own map he'll know where we've been previously. The colourful squiggles merge as I roll the trace into a translucent tube and hand it over.

Shortly after the Gurkhas depart the Herati Kandak also leave. This allows the British team to move into the American accommodation: two rows of metal shipping containers with a wooden door on the front, fitted with an air-con blower. CSM Johnstone is jubilant to at last be away from the dust as we cram our kit into the tiny room. We've got two other blokes in with us so it's a tight fit.

I've not yet arranged my kit when I'm struck down again with diarrhoea and vomiting. To guard against its spread through our ultra-close living quarters I'm isolated – sent back, with unwelcome irony, to our deserted shack.

The compound is devoid of people. Only the sad remnants of our ramshackle bivi positions remain in the dust. The shack, now empty except for my mosquito net, rifle and some water bottles, is stiflingly hot. Suddenly agitated, I smash the wall with the sole of my boot until one of the sheets of plywood splinters free of its nails and flops outwards. The air remains still. Sitting uneasily on a wooden pallet, I guzzle mineral water mixed with sachets of Gatorade, left by the Americans, to replace the water I'm losing with my twice-hourly bouts of liquid shitting.

The doctor brings over another sickie – Lance Corporal Bow who, like me, is well practised at diarrhoea and vomiting. As I'm no longer puking the doctor gives me more antibiotic pills, and tells me to continue eating to flush the bacteria out of my body.

As the sun sets I put my mossie net outside, hoping for a still night. I'm pleased to have some company. Lance Corporal Bow doesn't have much to say but he is, as ever, cheerful. He's blissfully unaware of the futility of our presence here. The satisfaction from his day's work comes from getting the radios working. He's the essence of unquestioning dependability, quietly tolerant of illness, futility and danger. I respect him deeply.

The UAV team appear and practise their take-off procedure. One of them runs along and throws the little plane in the air while another fiddles with a control box. It rasps away and, a few minutes later, makes a crash landing into the far side of the compound.

Time passes in a vacuum, a cycle of drinking Gatorade and going to the toilet repeatedly. The only anticipation is the consistency of my next shit.

We're distracted from our tedious isolation by the arrival of a resupply convoy from Tombstone. Standing on the perimeter wall we watch the elongated snake of vehicles – British, American and Afghan – approach under a towering dust cloud.

The distant roaring of the vehicles is interrupted by the pounding *crump!* of a muffled explosion.

'Fuck! IED!'

We train our rifle sights onto the convoy. An Afghan vehicle is half-toppled over, listing on its right side, surrounded
by a swirl of smoke and frantic, scurrying figures. They're
about five hundred metres away and through my sight I can
see them pulling at the cab of the pick-up truck. The rest of
the convoy is static with their troops dismounting, checking
the area around their vehicles for more IEDs (improvised
explosive devices).

More ANA arrive on the scene in pick-up trucks packed
with soldiers clinging onto the back. They've come out from
the FOB presumably to assist the casualties and allow the
convoy to get moving again.

To the right of the wagon that's been hit is a small village,
a cluster of perhaps two dozen low mud compounds min-
gled with trees and surrounded by a few patchy green fields
of wheat.

The ANA, now dismounted, are making for the village in
an extended line of little jogging figures. A flurry of shots
crackles. As the ANA disappear among the houses the agitated popping of shots continues. This doesn't look good.

'Jesus, what are they doing, Corporal Bow?

'Dunno, boss. I think they're barking.'

'You're right, whoever planted the IED's not gonna be
hanging around in the village.'

The shooting continues for another few minutes. The
British Quick Reaction Force arrives in a pair of Snatch wagons and the convoy slowly moves forward. The ANA trickle
out of the village and remount their wagons, joining the convoy. The two Snatch wagons remain static, guarding the

smashed ANA vehicle, waiting for an American Humvee to come and drag it into the camp.

Once recovered, and returned from my isolation, I go over to see HQ Company. It's still my job to supposedly 'mentor' Captain Hameed, but in reality, because they're such a small group and they're just manning the watchtowers, all I can do is pay social visits and hope to advise him.

As I enter the little office Captain Hameed greets me with a smile. I'm pleased to find Abdul Qadir, the company second-in-command, is also present, newly returned from his leave. He was in the convoy that got IED'd but happily is unscathed. We settle down on the matted floor to drink tea and nibble the sweet Panjshiri raisins he's brought with him from home. Captain Hameed tells me there were three ANA casualties from the IED, and by God's mercy no one died.

'And in the village?' I ask. 'Were there any casualties there?'

'Maybe,' he replies, unconcerned. 'These people are all against us. If they attack us, we must attack them.'

'But surely that makes the problem worse. If you speak to them, they may give you information to help us.'

He remains unconvinced. 'They do not want to help us. They are all criminals.'

I want to shout him down, but it's not a good time to be discussing hearts-and-minds tactics when they're clearly upset. An awkward silence falls on our little circle.

Keen to change the subject, I turn to Abdul Qadir. 'How is the Panjshir valley and how is your baby daughter?'

'Thanks be to God, she is well,' he replies, a warm smile

spreading across his face. 'And the trees at home are full of fruit.'

Ramadan enters with a basin. Onto aluminium plates he doles out big splodges of reddish sticky rice, and passes them round. Though simple, it's delicious. The interior wall facing me holds a slogan, elegantly scrawled in white chalk. Around it, little pink roses hang from the cracks in the rough mud plaster finish. As the others chatter, I ask Suhail, a Pashtun interpreter accompanying me in Tamim's place, what it means.

'It's saying that it was the Shura-e-Nazar who defeated the Soviets, so they can beat anyone. It is a slogan of the Tajik Northern Alliance . . . one of the Mujahideen groups.'

He speaks quietly, unwilling to be drawn into a sectarian discussion.

As we work our way through the stodgy rice with our fingers, a rifle shot cracks outside. Our actions frozen, we look up from our rice, mystified. Captain Hameed jumps up and rushes outside.

'Probably an ND [negligent discharge] – you know, an accident,' I say flatly.

A minute later, Captain Hameed returns, settling back down in the circle. 'A man has been killed, in the mosque, shot in the face. I'm not sure if it was on purpose.'

As he plunges his fingers back into his rice, we silently follow suit and resume our lunch.

Leaving the office, Suhail and I pass the mosque doorway, a few metres away. I look through the door. A squatting group of ANA soldiers stare silently at a green canvas sheet hiding the corpse. A blue-black puddle shrouds one end. It does not move me, perhaps because I can't see him. I want to lift the sheet and see the man's face – I imagine it must be caved in – to make it more real, and test its impact.

As we walk back to the other side of the FOB, we see the vehicle blown up by the IED, dumped at the side of the track. The rear half is shredded: a mangled mess of punctured metal. Shrapnel holes are scattered across the cab; the passengers, though gravely injured, are clearly very lucky to be alive. It's perverse that the soldiers in this pick-up survived and yet one has just been killed accidentally in the mosque.

Back at the accommodation containers I avoid a big group of officers chatting around a home-made picnic bench. A few more Captains arrived with the resupply convoy and there's not really anything for them to do. They've come up from Tombstone only because they're bored – especially Jim, who's had the good grace not to ask for his holster back.

Sitting down to chat with CSM Johnstone, I tell him about my lunch, but he's not interested. He went with the Quick Reaction Force to assist the convoy after the IED and saw Captain Hameed in the village.

'I seen him knock doon an old man. This old boy had a bag o' peas, and Capt'n Hameed ripped it frae his hand and punched him in the face. Knocked him clean over. It was fuckin' shockin' . . .'

'You're right,' I reply, sighing with resignation.

Inwardly I scoff at the recollection of arguing while on patrol about our troops walking through a field of wheat.

CHAPTER 10

Desert of Death

June 2006: Helmand Province, Afghanistan

Now in Camp Tombstone, I've a whole day to kill before going over to Camp Bastion and getting the Herc to Kabul and then a flight to Brize Norton. R&R! Ten days of 'rest and recuperation' in the UK. 'Fucking bring it on!' is my new whispered mantra. I'm chuffed to bits; I had avoided thinking about it until the moment I was told to be on the next Chinook out of Sangin.

In the dry sterility of Tombstone, I struggle to prevent my imagination making sudden flights of delicious fantasy about seeing Lucy and gorging on champagne. I'm determined not to believe that it's definitely happening until I'm actually on the RAF's Tristar, taking off from Kabul, as the R&R flights are infamous for savage delays.

At supper I revel in the fresh fruit and salads. The crunchy iceberg lettuce is a delectable treat after the monotony of bland MREs and Afghan rice.

Our dormitory is only half occupied now, by a bunch of officers mentoring an ANA logistics battalion. The occupants of the beds around my top bunk are all in Sangin. Their excess kit and personal effects remain in an odd assortment on top of their beds. I'm right in anticipating that on the lower bunk next to mine Jim, still in Sangin, has left his mini DVD-player at the top of one of his plastic trunks. Having arranged the little player on the dusty shelving unit, I stretch out in a camp chair and am completely absorbed by two hours of Napoleonic seafaring heroics.

Rising before the sun, I run rings around the inside of the perimeter. I'm hopelessly craving R&R now that it's suddenly here. Trudging around the little camp I can think only of Lucy. Now remembered, her face dominates my every thought, like a genie free of its bottle.

Having showered, I pull on my combats, a clean spare set.

One of the young officers from the logistics unit comes up and blurts out, 'Jim was killed last night. With two others . . . There was a contact.'

'Fuck . . .' is all I can manage in reply.

My stomach lurches and starts to fall. Sitting down, I put on my boots. Slowly buckling on my holster – *his* holster – I walk over to the operations room.

'The UAV crashed west of the river and the Gurkhas went to recover it. That was late last night,' the watchkeeper tells me in his soft Welsh tone.

'They got contacted and couldn't move so the Quick Reaction Force went out to give them a hand but got ambushed here.' He points to a map on the wall: there's a big red pin near a thin blue line, the Helmand River, just above a rash of black dots marking Sangin town.

'That's when Capt'n Phillipson got shot . . . Shot in the face.'

'Fuck,' I whisper to myself

'They got his body back to the FOB and then went out again to try to reach the Gurkhas, this time up to the north,' he continues, tracing the line of direction with a pencil point on the map. 'But they got ambushed again and the UAV Sergeant Major lost an arm, blown off by an RPG, and a Corporal was shot in the chest but he's all right. At that stage Apache went up and the 105 guns in the FOB fired. The Paras sent out B Company from Camp Bastion to help everyone extract. So they're all back in the FOB now and the Paras are in the town.'

'What about the ANA, did they go out with the QRF?' I ask.

'They went out but when it kicked off they bolted and left their wagons with the lights on and engines running, so the Taliban fuckin' stole 'em,' he replies quietly.

In the dormitory I return the DVD-player to the plastic trunk, carefully replacing a *Wild Geese* disc into the player, leaving it as I found it. The trunk contains a stash of cards from his family. There's one of a silly cartoon dog from his mother. With a falling sensation in my stomach I quickly close the lid and go outside.

Over at the interpreters' hut I seek news of Tamim; he should be back from his leave by now. From a sitting circle of interpreters drinking tea, one of them rises and tells me that his return is unlikely.

'Captain, he will not come back, he has gone home to be married.'

'I didn't think it was happening so soon,' I reply, thinking, surely Tamim would have told me about it?

'Well, take his number and give him a call,' he continues. He scrawls a string of digits into my notebook, copied from his mobile phone. Declining his offer of tea I thank him and leave.

Back in the dormitory I clean my rifle; it'll stay in the armoury while I'm on R&R. A Sergeant Major comes in and asks which is Captain Phillipson's bedspace. I show him. Unfolding a big brown cardboard box he packs the contents of the bedspace into it. By the time I've finished cleaning my rifle, the Sergeant Major has left with the box and the bedspace is empty.

In the afternoon I'm over at Camp Bastion waiting for the flight to Kabul. Walking through the lines of yellow half-cylindrical tents, a 3 Para officer I know from Sandhurst passes and greets me. He's excited about an imminent arrest operation.

'We're out a bit later after some high-value targets. It's bound to go noisy.'

'What planet are you on?' I think, as I wish him good luck. This is not a game, a chance to fulfil personal fighting fantasies. If we want a fight we'll get one here, a thousand times over, but to what end? Violence will surely breed more violence, until the whole thing is beyond our control.

The shock of the morning's news has compressed my frustration into anger. I want very badly to talk about the whole thing, to share it and be told that sense will now prevail, at the tragic price of this death.

The Camp's headquarters is a quadrangle of low canvas tents and elaborate radio antennae encircled by a thick earthen barrier. Passing the gate guard, I enter one of the tents through a door flap into a stuffy interior, yellow under fluorescent tube lights. Keen to find out what we're going to do, now that disaster has struck, I find the liaison officer responsible for our team. He's our link to this headquarters and has been relaying the orders to us from Helmand Task Force HQ in Lashkar Gah.

'What's the form?' I ask, approaching his desk. 'Are we pulling out of Sangin or what?'

'Mmm, no. One of the Para companies is going to stay on at the District Centre. Other than that the plan's not really changed, Leo.'

'What plan?' I retort, flashing with anger. 'There is no plan . . . We fucking well made it up as we went along going into Sangin, you know that.'

'Easy, mucker, it's not my fault this has happened,' he says plaintively.

'This is fucking nonsense. We blundered into that town not even knowing where our objective was, and we've sat there like a bloody great target doing fuck-all.'

'Mate, chill,' he says standing and raising his palms

'Don't tell me to fucking chill!' I want to grab his pasty white face and smash it on the desk between us. 'This is a fucking disgrace! More blokes'll die up there, for no reason, and we're doing fuck-all about it.'

Flushing red, he sits back down and looks intently at his computer screen. Other officers in the tent glance awkwardly at me. I'm making a scene. Breathing heavily I turn about, push past the canvas door flap and leave, angered even more now by my lack of eloquence.

In the large tented cookhouse I make myself tea in a polystyrene cup. The Sky News headlines flash in noisy repetition across a TV screen, watched by a few off-duty blokes wearing PT kit and flip-flops, their weapons lying next to their chairs.

'First British Soldier Killed in Helmand' comes up in bold, above a simple map of the Province with 'Sangin' enlarged on a red pointing arrow, followed by some archive footage from somewhere in northern Afghanistan. The soldier's anonymity means his parents are still uninformed. The camp's internet and phone cabin is still closed with an 'op minimise' sign on the door, in order to prevent those in camp communicating his name to the media before his parents have the news. This unintentionally provides all other parents of those in Helmand, aware that an unnamed soldier has been killed, with ample opportunity to imagine that their child is dead. The suspense of waiting can only end when someone else's son has their photo flashed up on the news, and the collective trauma of anticipation is passed onto a few individuals whose lives are shattered.

Sick of the Sky News intro music, I move outside and join the crowd for the pre-flight roll call. The gathered troops are jubilant to be leaving for R&R and banter boisterously until a voluntary hush falls as a list of ranks and names is called out and each one is claimed by a shouted reply.

As we wait for a brief from the logistics corporal, I chat to an Artillery CSM whom I know from the first operation going into Sangin; he rode in the back of Sergeant Stoddart's dilapidated ANA wagon. He left Sangin on the same Chinook as me and is disappointed.

'Gutted to have missed it, boss,' he says as we talk quietly.

I know he's not being macho, he really means it. We both know that it will have inflicted on most of the participants one of the most intense experiences of their lives so far, and for some the worst experience ever – seeing a friend shot through the face. Because of this and despite this it holds a tragic allure for near-miss non-participants. He's done probably twenty years in the Army and yet as a professional soldier still craves opportunities to risk everything and relish life through avoiding death.

I know he really means it because I feel the same. I'm angry at the death of a friend and know that it marks the arrival of catastrophe for his family, the people of Sangin, and the British and Afghan soldiers in Helmand, and yet I feel guilty for my absence when CSM Johnstone and everyone else was in the thick of it. I've missed out for not having been there, in the fatal contact. My anger is contradictory, and this compounds my anger.

In Kabul the tedious checking-in procedure is repeated for the Tristar flight to Brize Norton. A nurse escorts a man to the check-in desk; he's dressed in trainers, jeans and a colourful shirt, with his left arm now a fat cocoon of immaculate white bandage. He's the CSM from the UAV team, a casualty of the fatal contact. He recognises me and we chat briefly.

His gruff Mancunian voice is very chirpy. 'I reckon I'll get at least two hundred grand in compensation for this,' he says, pointing his chin to the stump. 'I'm fockin' made!'

On the plane, I stare out of the port-side window, struggling to avoid conversing with an over-friendly officer from ISAF headquarters.

'How's it going in Helmand?' he asks

'It's a disaster,' I reply, staggered that he doesn't already know this.

'A catastrophe,' I continue, as he widens his eyes in surprise. 'We've blundered into Sangin and other places and achieved fuck-all . . . The whole reconstruction bit is just nonsense, it's non-existent on the ground, it's just not there. Going into the north is a blunder, a full-on military blunder and all the blokes can do now is fight to survive.'

He's taken aback by my response and the conversation dies. Disconsolate, I resume my window-staring in silence. After so much uncertainty over the previous months, certain truths are now starkly clear. I know that this is the start of terrible violence and that we've lost this campaign before it's even started. I know that soldiers dying in Helmand is pointless. I know that our artillery shells and Apache helicopters will, in a tragic replay of Soviet clumsiness, kill countless Afghan civilians while pursuing a nebulous enemy. I feel foolish for believing so wholeheartedly that in coming to Afghanistan I would be part of something intelligent, meaningful and constructive. I know now that our entry into Helmand has been ignorant, clumsy and destructive – a vainglorious folly.

My faith in the establishment to which I have devoted my life for more than five years has proved to be ill-founded. I feel angry at this betrayal, and angry at my own foolishness. A feeling – not a decision, but a slowly rising knowledge – comes to me that I will leave the Army and voice my anger.

The Hindu Kush spreads below us, an unending carpet of miniature brown peaks. Casting my mind back to Rich Holmes's funeral, I swear at the thought of more funerals to come.

*

With the death of Captain Jim Phillipson, Sangin exploded into violence. The District Centre, occupied by the Parachute Regiment, became the scene of the fiercest fighting experienced by the British Army since the Korean war.

In late June Captain David Patten and Sergeant Paul Bartlett were killed near FOB Robinson.

In early July Corporal Peter Thorpe and Lance Corporal Jabron Hashmi were killed on the roof of the Sangin District Centre and Private Damian Jackson was killed in the town.

In August Corporal Bryan Budd was killed in the town during an action for which he was posthumously awarded the Victoria Cross.

In September Lance Corporal Luke McCulloch was killed in the town.

*

London, October 2006. The Major General's door is unmoving. In a sweaty state of trepidation I replay back and forth the events of the last few weeks.

After returning from Afghanistan I headed off alone to travel across Asia, using the three months' 'terminal' leave due to me at the end of my service. Just before departing, however, I spoke to a journalist about Afghanistan. I was forthright; I told her exactly what I thought of the situation, and about my personal decision to leave the Army.

Ten days later I was buying horses in Kazakhstan, cutting a deal with a toothless farmer for a pair of stocky ponies that I intended to ride the length of the country into neighbouring Uzbekistan.

'I'll be back tomorrow to collect,' I told the chuckling farmer, as I handed over grubby wads of the local currency.

Dossing down that night in the house of an American Peace Corps worker whom I'd met in the local town, I checked my e-mail – the last opportunity to do so for probably a couple of months. Stacked with messages, my in-box told a frantic chronology of events. The write-up of my interview with the journalist had made the front page of last weekend's *Sunday Times*, with my picture splashed across the front page of its *News Review* section. On the following days the story had become front-page news in the rest of the national press and had also been seized upon by American and international networks. I was amazed by the magnitude of interest generated by a member of the Army publicly criticising the campaign in Afghanistan. Perhaps Kazakhstan wasn't remote enough for me to get away with breaking Army rules that forbid speaking to the media.

A dozen e-mails from the likes of ITN News and *The Today Programme* requested interviews and another dozen, mostly from fellow officers serving in Afghanistan and Iraq, offered support. There were also a couple from the furious Scots Guards Adjutant. 'Where are you? You must return to London immediately' was followed by: 'Telephone the Commanding Officer now ... The longer you ignore this message, the more serious the consequences.'

Twenty-four hours later I was on an Air Astana flight bound for Amsterdam, having resold the ponies to the toothless farmer to his utter delight and considerable gain, and spent the cash on the airfare. I'd weighed up the odds and decided against doing a runner; I didn't want to be declared 'absent without leave' and face arrest on my eventual return to the UK, as hinted at by the Scots Guards Com-

manding Officer when I spoke to him on a crackling Peace
Corps satellite phone:

'This has made waves at a ministerial level ... The Chief of
the Defence Staff has personally demanded your retrieval ...'

Landing at London Gatwick, bearded and filthy in my riding breeches, I returned immediately to Wellington Barracks
to be charged with misconduct. I'd broken the rules by
expressing my opinion on the British strategy in Afghanistan, to the possible detriment of that campaign, went the
official line.

For the next month I endured the tedious machinations of
the Army's disciplinary system. I explained myself repeatedly, an investigation was made, and professional reports and
character references were gathered from various sources.
Finally my case file was ready to go before the Major General for his judgement.

The Aide-de-Camp answers the phone again. This time
it's from next door.

'The General will see you now,' says the ADC, gesturing
with a forced smile towards the tall oak door.

Moving into the huge and richly furnished office, I close
the door softly behind me. Slamming my heels left-right
onto the floor, I stand to attention in a formal halt before the
Major General's desk.

'Leo, how nice to see you,' says the Major General, without
irony. A rangy giant of a man, his charm and good humour
are legendary throughout the Foot Guards. For a moment
I'm also really pleased to see him, before assuming a face of
contrition.

He opens my case file: an inch-thick stack of papers in a

lever-arch folder. Pulling it free of its binding, he arranges the different annexes before him, his long artistic fingers nudging them into a well-ordered line across the desk top. Full-length portraits of William and Mary stare down at us from behind the Major General. I glance at the red handkerchief billowing from the breast pocket of his dark suit; I'm glad I'm equally well dressed.

'Of course you understand the magnitude of this,' he says, looking up and pulling off his glasses. 'Just how, exactly, did it happen?'

I explain, with frankness, well practised now after a month of repetition.

The Major General nods. 'So your views are, would you say, correctly represented in this article?' he asks, his fingers coming to rest on the *Sunday Times News Review*. I can see my bearded face upside down on its cover.

'Yes, sir, verbatim.' I like him but I feel no regret at all. Perhaps he even *agrees* with me?

'I have little choice but to give you a Letter of Censure . . . The impact of which would of course be much greater were you not leaving the service.'

'Yes, sir,' I reply solemnly. Inwardly I'm not bothered; it means I couldn't command the Scots Guards were I to stay in the Army and I'm barred from joining the Foreign Office, but I'd sooner drive a bus.

'It would be very unfortunate if this were to appear in the media,' the Major General continues softly.

'Yes, sir,' I reply.

'Given that you've waited a month for this interview you may, I think, resume your leave.'

'Thank you very much, sir,' I reply, allowing the hint of a smile to appear. I'm *sure* he agrees with the article.

'You will return to Asia?'

'Yes, sir.'

Emerging into the autumn sun on Horse Guards Parade, I loosen my tie and breath deeply. I know that I'll head east again, as soon as possible, but only after I've set down a few things in writing.

Postcript. CSM Tommy Johnstone, of the Army Air Corps, was Mentioned in Despatches for his bravery while serving in Helmand Province.

Epilogue

Since the first British soldier was killed in action in Sangin in June 2006, the violence sweeping Helmand Province has killed dozens of British soldiers and hundreds of their Afghan National Army colleagues. Countless Afghan civilians have died in the crossfire, Afghan homes lie ruined by British artillery shells and opium production is at an all-time high. The British intervention in Helmand Province has been not only a blundering catastrophe, but a violent tragedy. It is still unfolding as I write.

The soldiers of the Helmand Task Force are suffering a ferocious enemy onslaught in the northern towns of Sangin, Naw Zad, Musa Qala and Kajaki and in the southern town of Garmsir. More than fifty servicemen have been killed and eighty-five wounded in action. Currently, small groups of soldiers are still fighting and dying in these locations.

These troops, under great pressure, have been unswervingly professional and brave. Sadly they are the unfortunate victims of strategic confusion generated by a command hierarchy that is unworthy of their trust.

When, in late 2005, the UK agreed to intervene in Helmand Province as part of NATO's increased engagement with Afghanistan, the challenge could not have been greater. For the previous four years, since the fall of the Taliban, Helmand (like most other provinces lying beyond the reach of the fledgling government in Kabul) had been left untouched by any form of central governance. Opium barons and lawlessness held sway.

The plan at the outset of the British deployment into Helmand in April 2006 was based around a 'comprehensive approach'. Well-documented in British military doctrine, the essence of this approach is that the military must act in concert with other players to achieve results. Another doctrinal inspiration was the 'inkspot' strategy, relating to a successful counter-insurgency conducted by the British in Malaya in the 1950s.

The plan was simple: within an inkspot haven of security the comprehensive approach would be established to nurture civil development and governance. Three lines of operation – security, development and governance – were to run concurrently, all interdependent and of equal importance. The Army secures the inkspot, allowing the Department for International Development (DfID) to initiate development. The Foreign and Commonwealth Office (FCO) would help the Afghans govern themselves and, crucially, drive the counter-narcotics campaign. The overall effect would be the reconstruction of civil society.

Reconstruction is desperately needed as civil society has been all but destroyed by incessant violence in Afghanistan during the last thirty years. A decade of all-out war against the invading Soviet army was followed by inter-factional fighting among the victorious Mujahideen groups, the rise of the Taliban, and their removal by a US-led Coalition, allied to the Northern Alliance. This violence has left the population deeply traumatised, exploited by opium barons, and denied access to healthcare, education, justice and other fundamental provisions of a developed, civilised society.

The Helmand inkspot was to be a limited triangular area of operations based around the provincial capital Lashkar Gah, the nearby town of Gereshk, and the newly created hub of British operations, the dust-ridden and far-flung Camp Bastion.

While the three lines of operation are interdependent and must occur simultaneously, they must also, as a matter of course, be preceded by a rigorous intelligence assessment of the target area and possibly by some form of information campaign. The key to success is winning the hearts and minds of the civil population through tangible developmental improvements such as basic healthcare and education. As success is consolidated the inkspot slowly grows, on a timescale marked in years rather than months.

The insurgent will of course fight this process, but deprived of civilian sympathy and denied freedom of movement he will only manage occasional acts of terrorism within the inkspot. Overwhelming targeted violence is the just response to such a threat, because the safety of the civilian population and their trust in the security forces is quite simply the be-all and end-all of the entire strategy. High-intensity war-fighting on a broad front, with civilians dying as collateral damage, is therefore a nightmare scenario of failure. Tragically this has come to pass in Helmand.

In the early stages of the deployment a spectacular digression from the comprehensive approach was made: the British command deployed small teams of British and Afghan troops to occupy remote northern towns of the Province.

These teams were deployed despite the fact that DfID and the FCO had absolutely no effective practical measures in place in northern Helmand. Two of the three lines of operation were missing. The troops, deployed in isolation, had no real means of winning hearts and minds; they could offer no practical developmental improvements and were unable to even state the British policy on opium production. Their presence soon became antagonistic; like honey-pot targets, they attracted anyone fancying a crack at the invading infidel, seemingly no better than the Russians before them.

Once attacked, these teams were quickly sucked into lethal high-intensity war-fighting, which is still raging. Over-exposed and often outgunned on the ground, British troops have had to rely on close air support (British Apache attack helicopters and American A10 'Tank-busters') and artillery (105mm guns). This escalation of violence is their primary means of survival. But these weapons are not the surgical tools best used by the counter-insurgent: they are blunt-edged, indiscriminate and have killed numerous civilians.

The decision to scatter small groups of soldiers across the north of Helmand, in isolation, in an intelligence vacuum and with complete disregard for the most basic tenets of counter-insurgency was, quite simply, a gross military blunder. Its exact provenance is uncertain, but it was probably the result of political pressure from London and Kabul, requests from the Provincial Governor keen to extend his authority, and an impatient overconfidence within the British command.

It would be absurd to suggest that war-fighting on a broad front, supposedly 'drawing out' the Taliban, is a necessary prelude to the reconstructive phases of the comprehensive approach. Violence begets violence, as thousands of new local recruits, previously uninterested in radical Islam, are drawn to the Taliban cause, hungry for revenge after civilian deaths in their communities.

Because of the failure to properly establish security any-where in Helmand, developmental reconstruction work is occurring nowhere. Without guaranteed personal safety, DfID and FCO personnel remain in their compounds, if indeed they are present at all. As the Governor of Helmand pointed out to the BBC in October 2006: 'Promises to get projects up and running have not been kept and there hasn't even been a DfID representative in Helmand for two months . . .'

Security cannot exist without development and develop-ment cannot begin without security. The Helmand Task Force is achieving neither.

Afghanistan produces 92 per cent of the world's opium. According to the United Nations' *Afghan Opium Survey 2006*, Helmand Province has a phenomenal 42 per cent share of that production. Poppy-growing *is* the economy and the livelihood of the vast majority of the rural population. Exploited by middlemen, these poor cash-croppers have no other choice. The opium industry is closely linked to fund-ing the Taliban. It is therefore incredible that the FCO failed to carry out any kind of *practical* counter-narcotics strategy at the start of the Helmand campaign. Despite counter-narcotics being a British responsibility for Afghanistan as a whole (under the Bonn agreement of 2001) there was, at the start of the campaign, no functional plan at the provincial level. Unless poppy-growers are informed about viable alternatives and what their future might hold, they will only assume that their livelihoods are under threat and react with hostility. Months into the campaign, senior planning officers in the Helmand Task Force headquarters were unable to articulate the British counter-narcotics plan. Meanwhile, the narco-economy is booming: by British Foreign Minister Kim Howells's own admission Helmand's poppy production hit a record high in 2006, with a staggering 162 per cent increase from the previous year.

The British face a broad spectrum of opposition in Helmand. The enemy cannot simply be described as 'Taliban'. A Helmand poppy-farmer can hang up his hoe over lunchtime, pick up his Kalashnikov, shoot at the British and be back in the fields for the rest of the afternoon. The farmer has nothing ideologically in common with the Taliban but they may share a common aim, for example the absence of foreign troops, for different motives. If the real enemy is hard to identify and looks very similar to local civilians, intelligence-gathering must compensate for this. Unfortunately, in the early stages of the deployment, in places like Sangin British troops suffered from a worrying lack of sound intelligence. This was due probably to the fact that the mechanisms in place for its gathering and analysis were run by desk-bound staff officers lacking field experience of

Afghanistan and devoid of reliable sources. The result was a dangerous ignorance of local tribal, political and social structures, and the intricate manner in which these interweave with Islamic radicalism and opium production.

Looking forward, I firmly believe that a smaller British military presence would be much less offensive and potentially more effective than a large conventional force. Small numbers of determined Afghan-experts, having spent years in the country and gained a profound knowledge of local culture, language and politics, might discreetly be able to guide the Afghans in solving their problems largely themselves. This approach has started in a very minor way; the bearded members of the operational mentoring teams seek to enhance the capability of the Afghan National Army. Their effectiveness is limited by the high turnover of personnel (in accordance with the British six-month tour cycle), but the improvement of the ANA is a sensible platform on which to base an eventual but very distant military exit strategy.

This 'discrete effect' approach should apply equally to the military's partners in the comprehensive approach. Counternarcotics and development must be driven forward in the field by risk-taking practical operators, disinclined to stay at their desks in Lashkar Gah or Kandahar.

Discrete effort inside Afghanistan will, however, be futile without action at the strategic, international level. Diplomacy beyond the porous and lawless border with Pakistan should aim to inhibit the opium market, and stem the flow of well-equipped young 'jihadis' desperate for martyrdom against NATO soldiers. Resolving these issues is a fundamental precursor to future success in Helmand Province.

The British forces in Helmand, unsupported by the other arms of government and plunged hastily into isolated peril, have lost the battle for hearts and minds before they had a proper chance to win. In 2006 more than 4,000 civilians were killed 'collaterally' in Afghanistan, many in Helmand. This lost ground will take a generation to regain.

We cannot fight our way to a solution. A peaceful, developed Helmand cannot be won by the sword, and the longer we try, the greater the tragedy.

Leo Docherty
March 2007